ADORABLE ELEPHANT DESIGNS

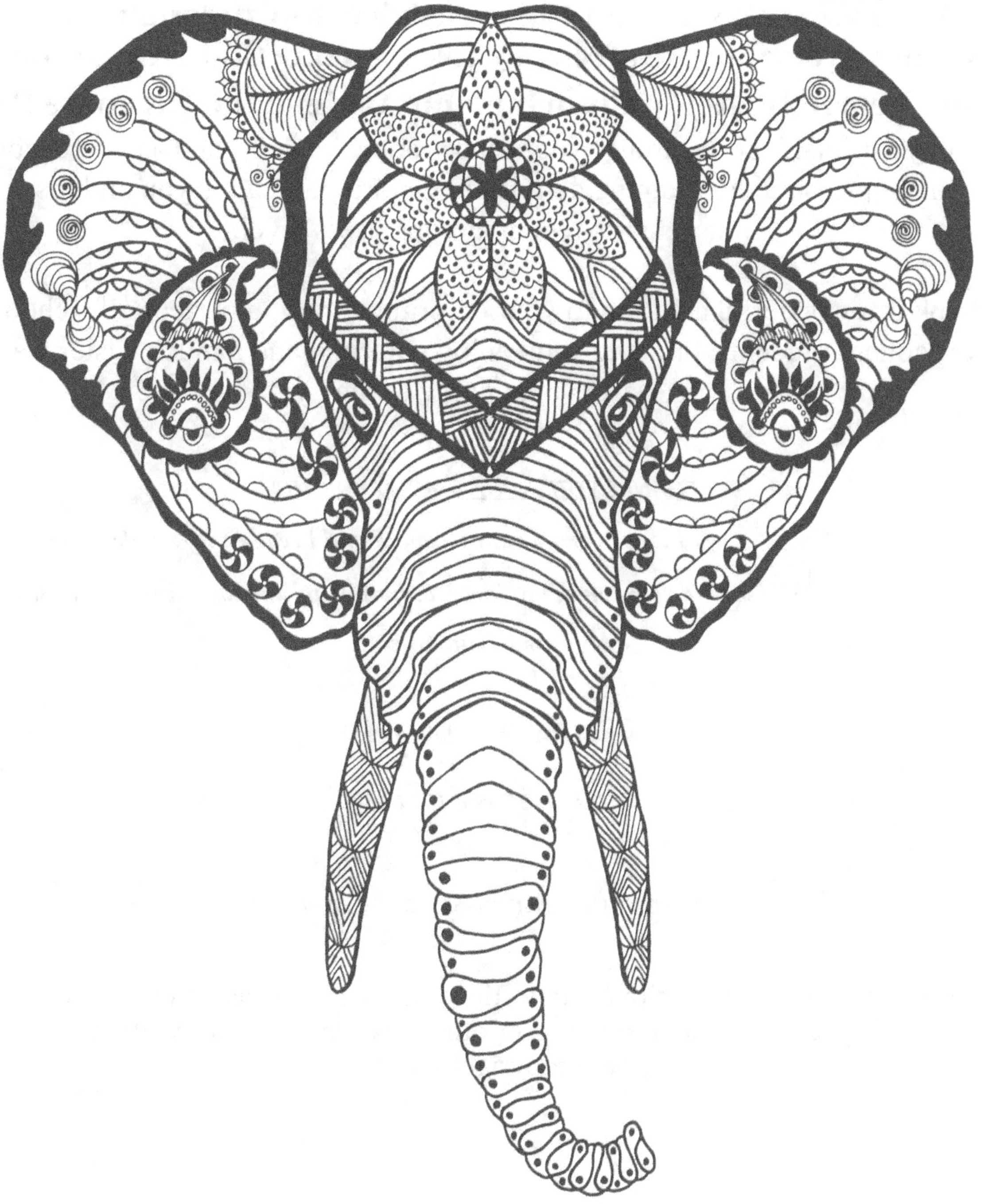

Adorable Elephant
Stress Relieving Elephant designs for Adult!

It is time you relax and let the creativity flow through you. Step away from everyday life stress by taking Your Coloring to the Next Level - Learn the Art of Coloring and Achieve the Ultimate Bliss!

Bring out your imagination, arouse your senses and creativity, and as you become engaged in the pleasurable, soothing activity of Coloring, it calms you and instantaneously starts reducing your stress level.

This book is a wonderful addition to your coloring library; a perfect gift school aged children, college students, or adults who enjoy coloring, and a much easier way to reduce stress than going to the gym.

THANKS YOU FOR YOUR PATRONAGE

I love hearing your feedback and I read every single review

Please send your comment, ideas, compliments and anything else to me at:

stevojionu@gmail.com

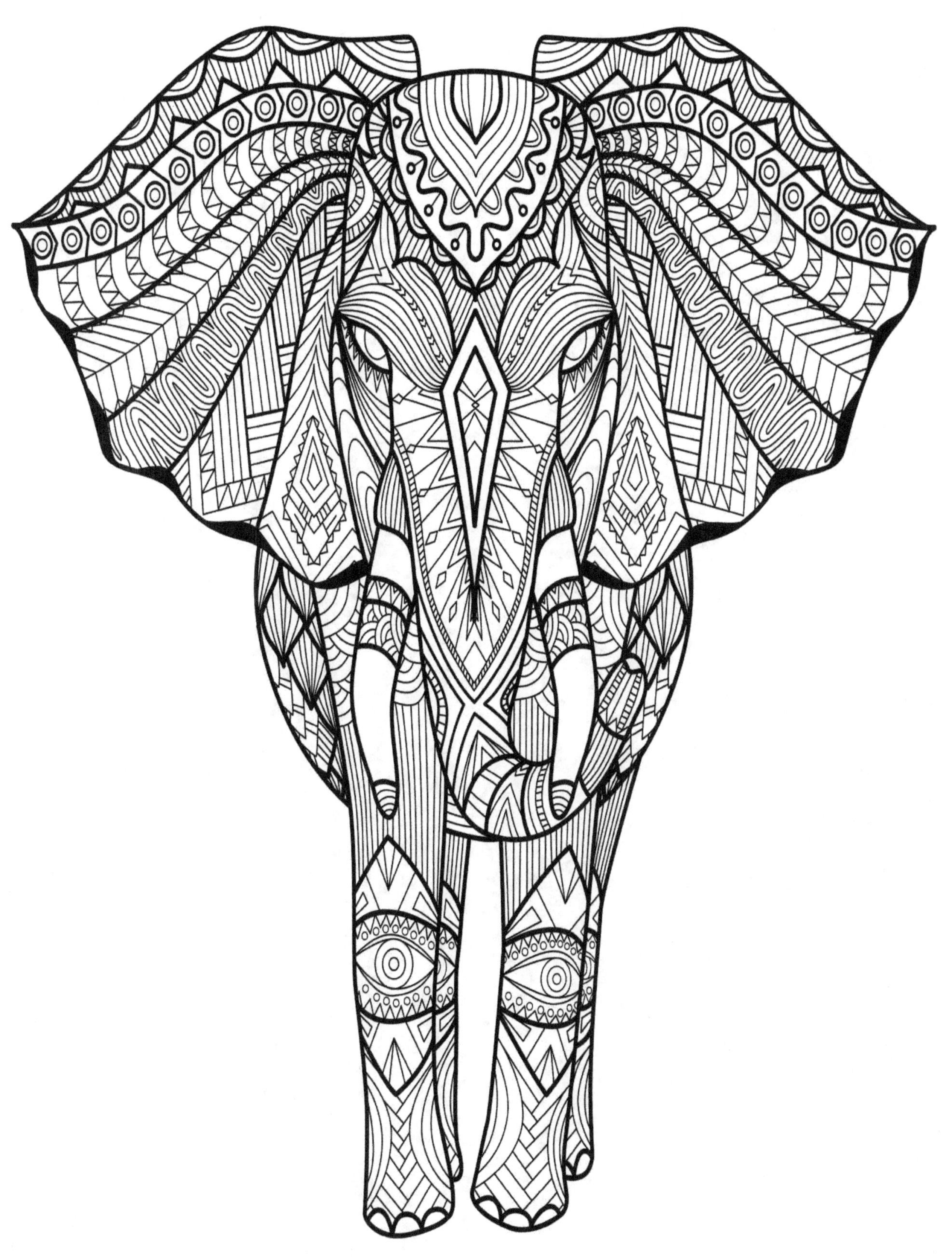

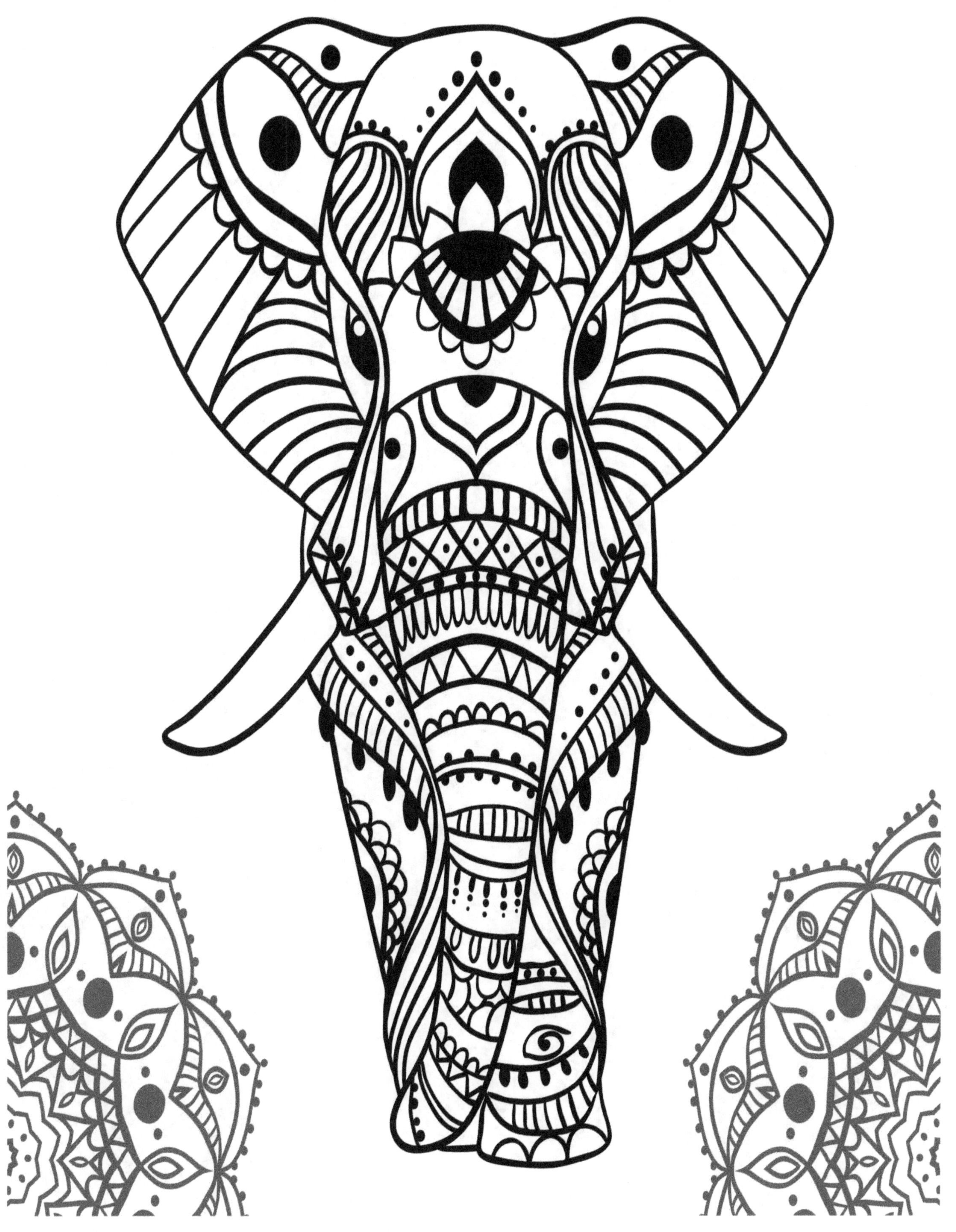

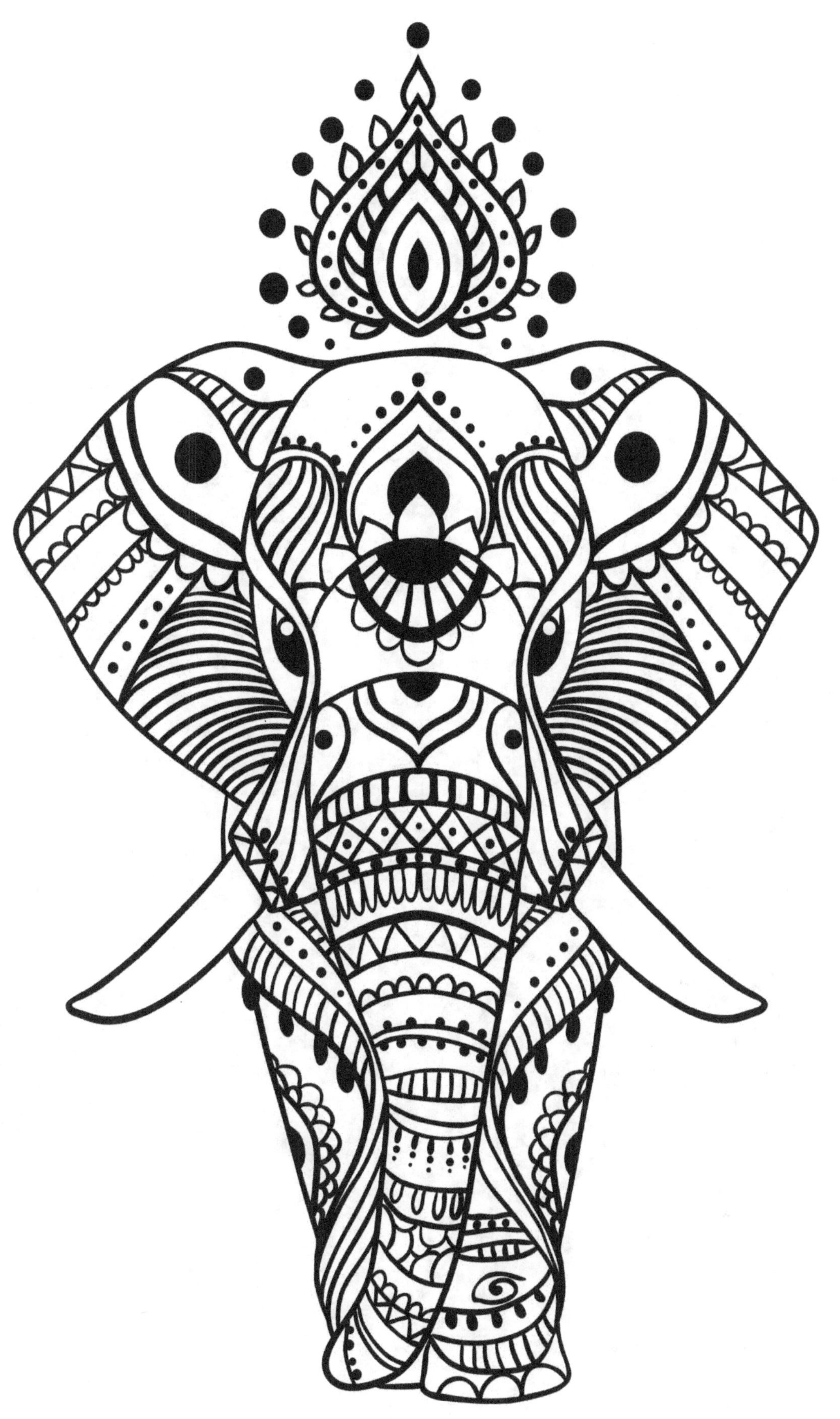

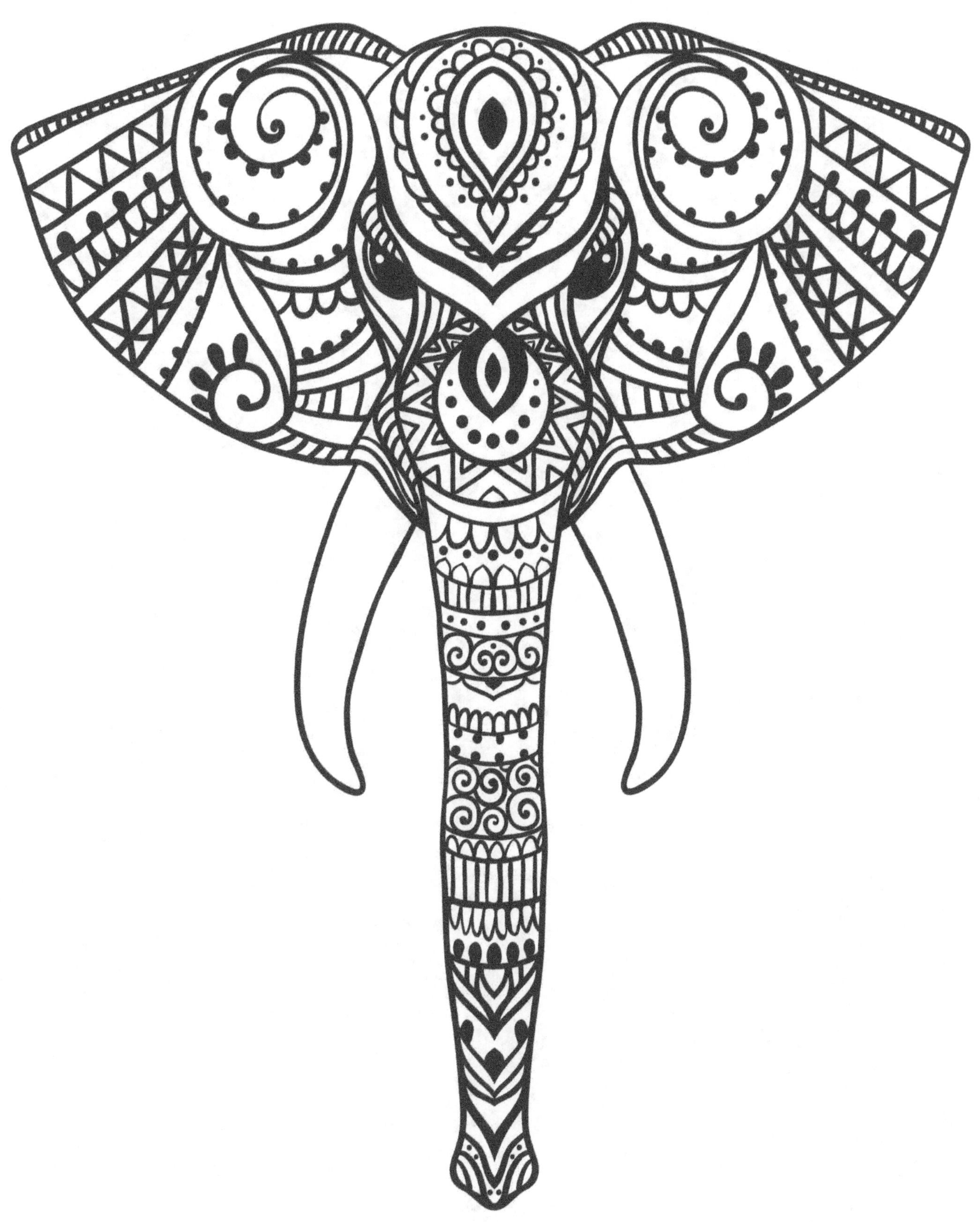

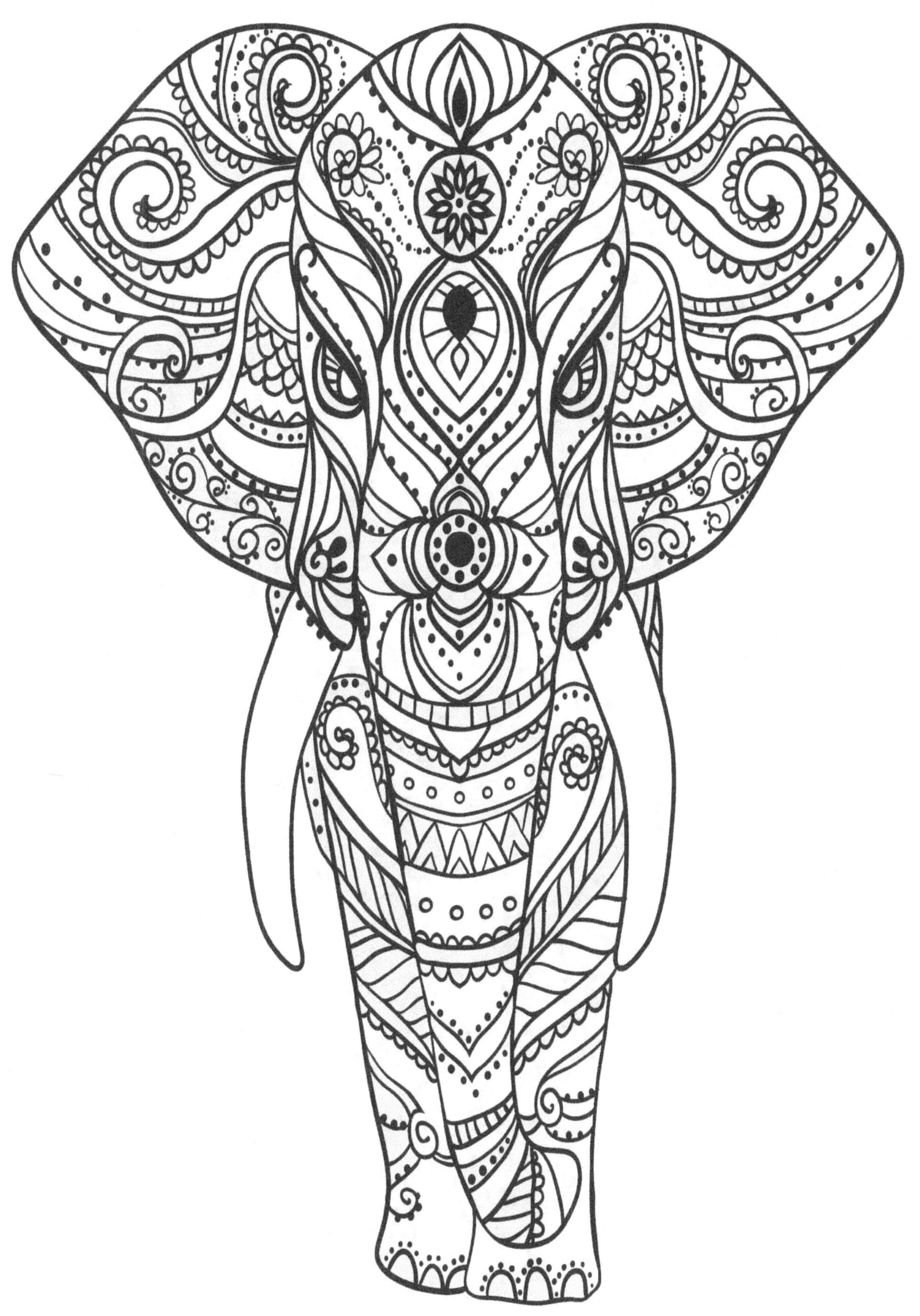

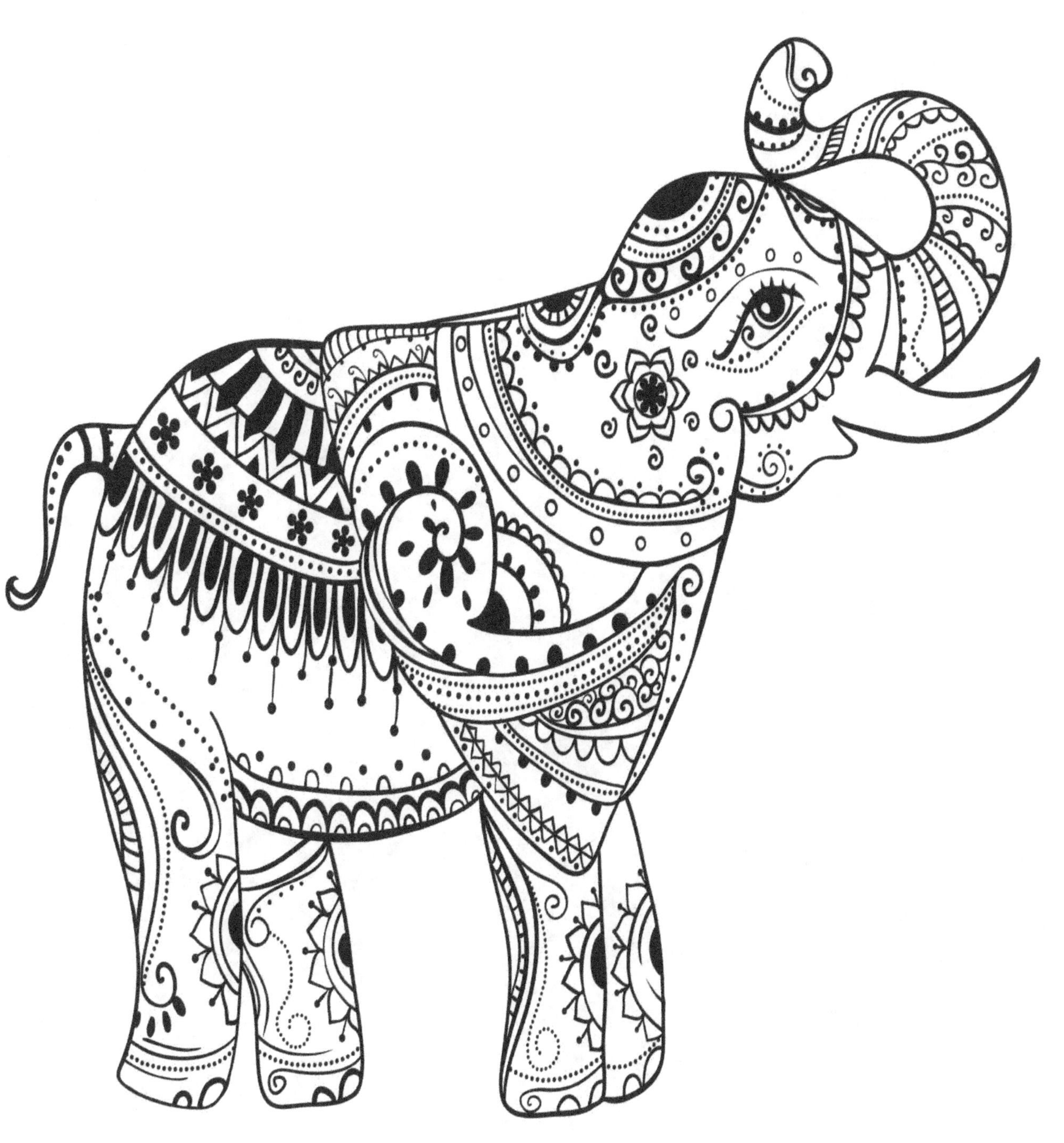

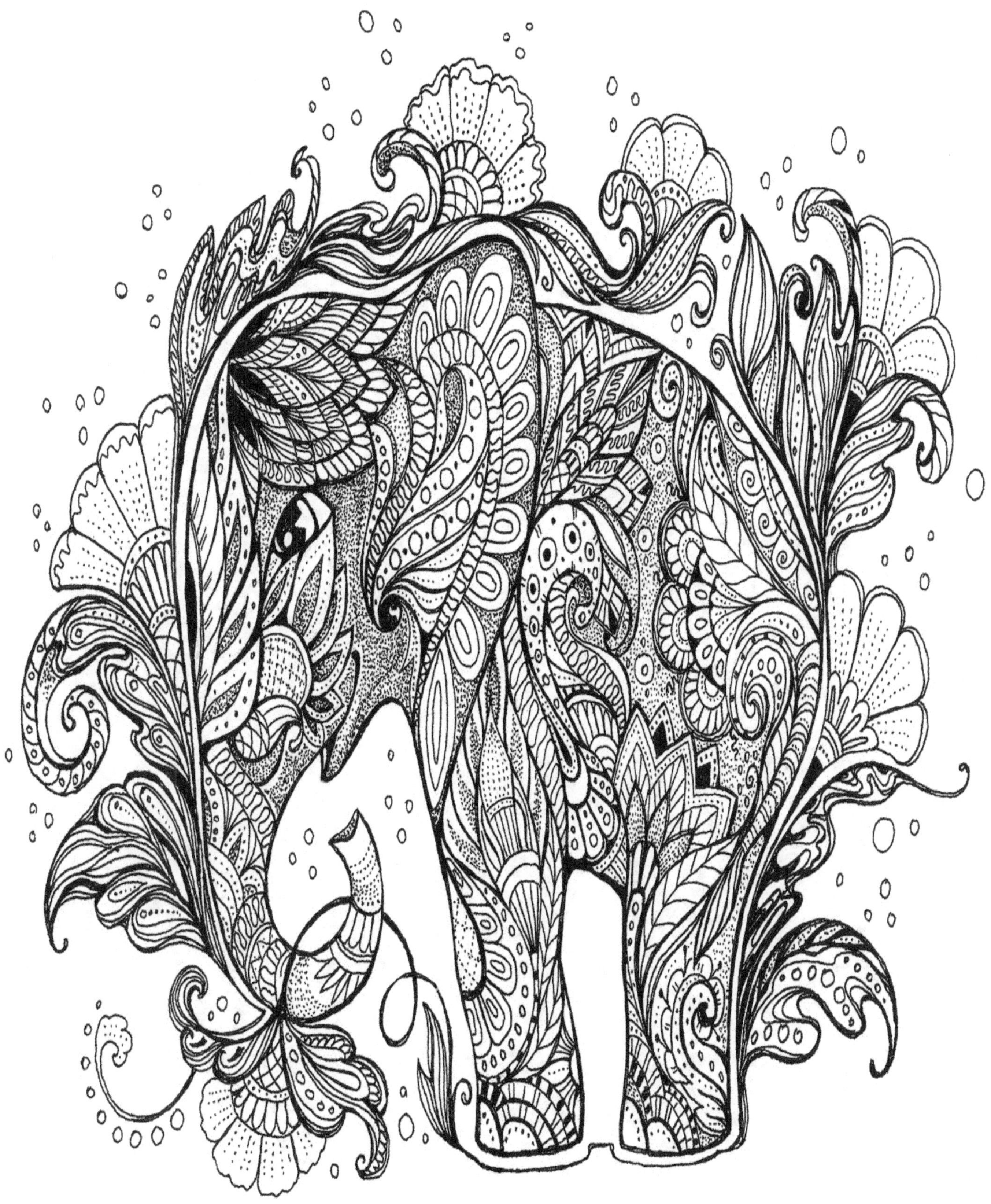

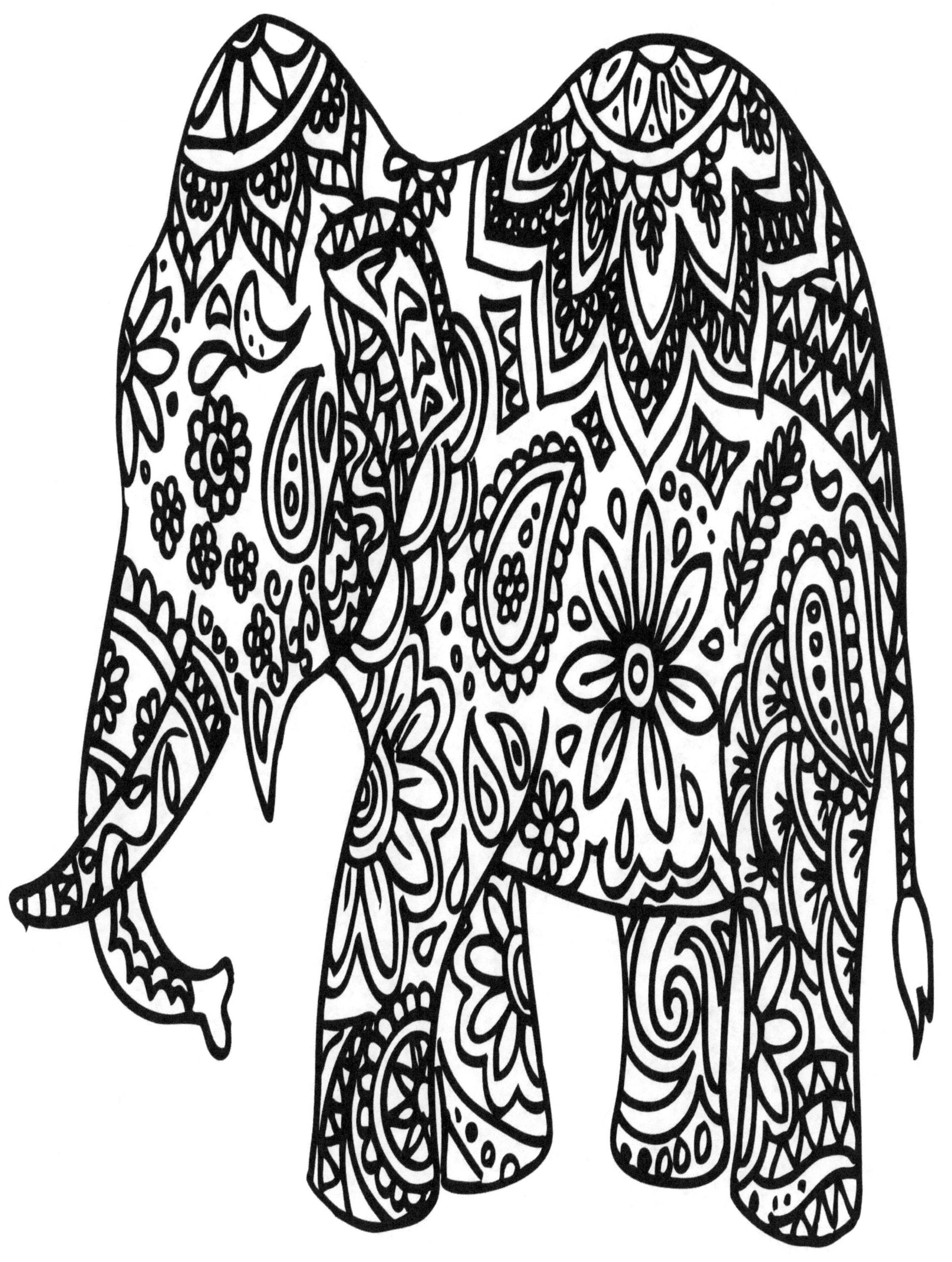

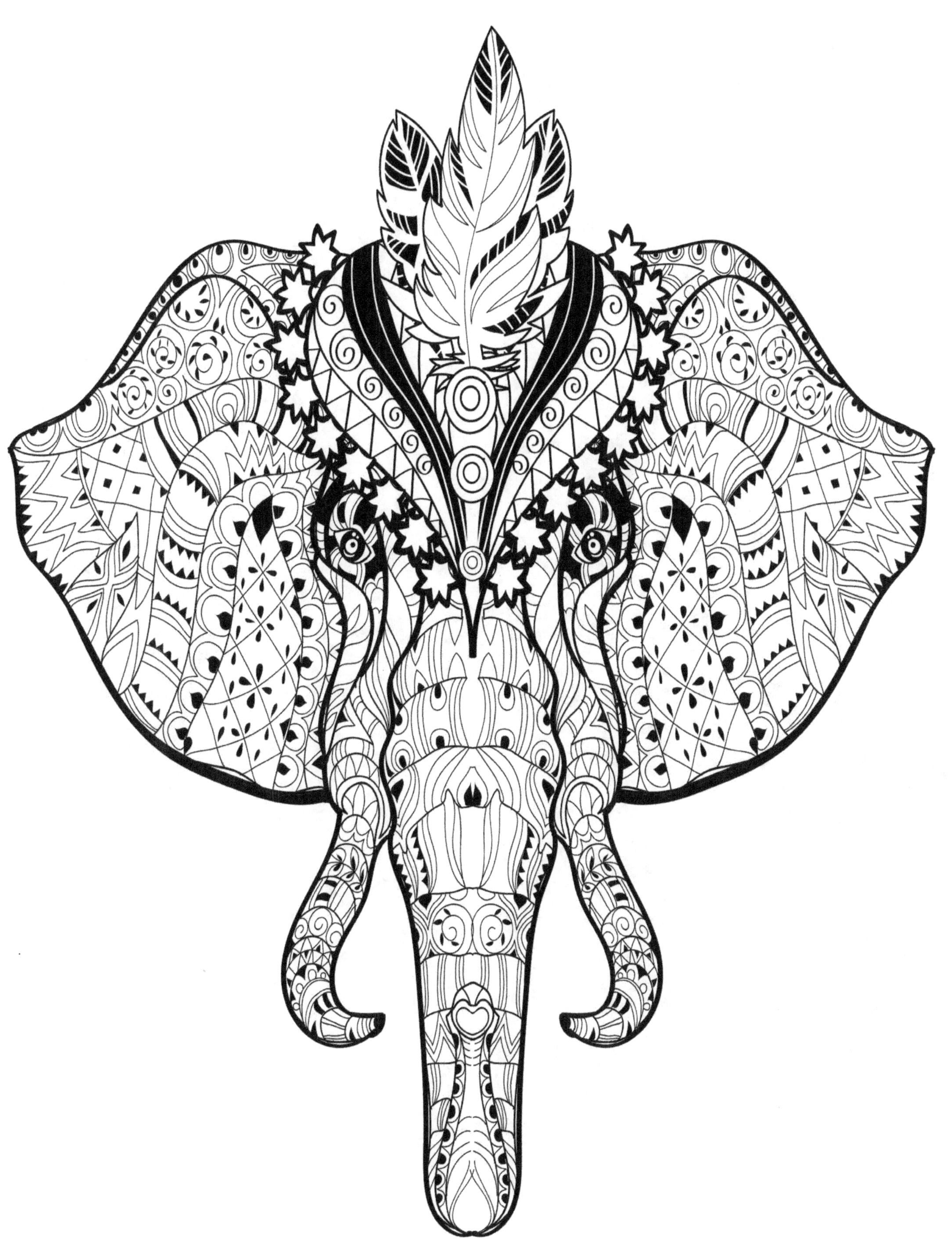

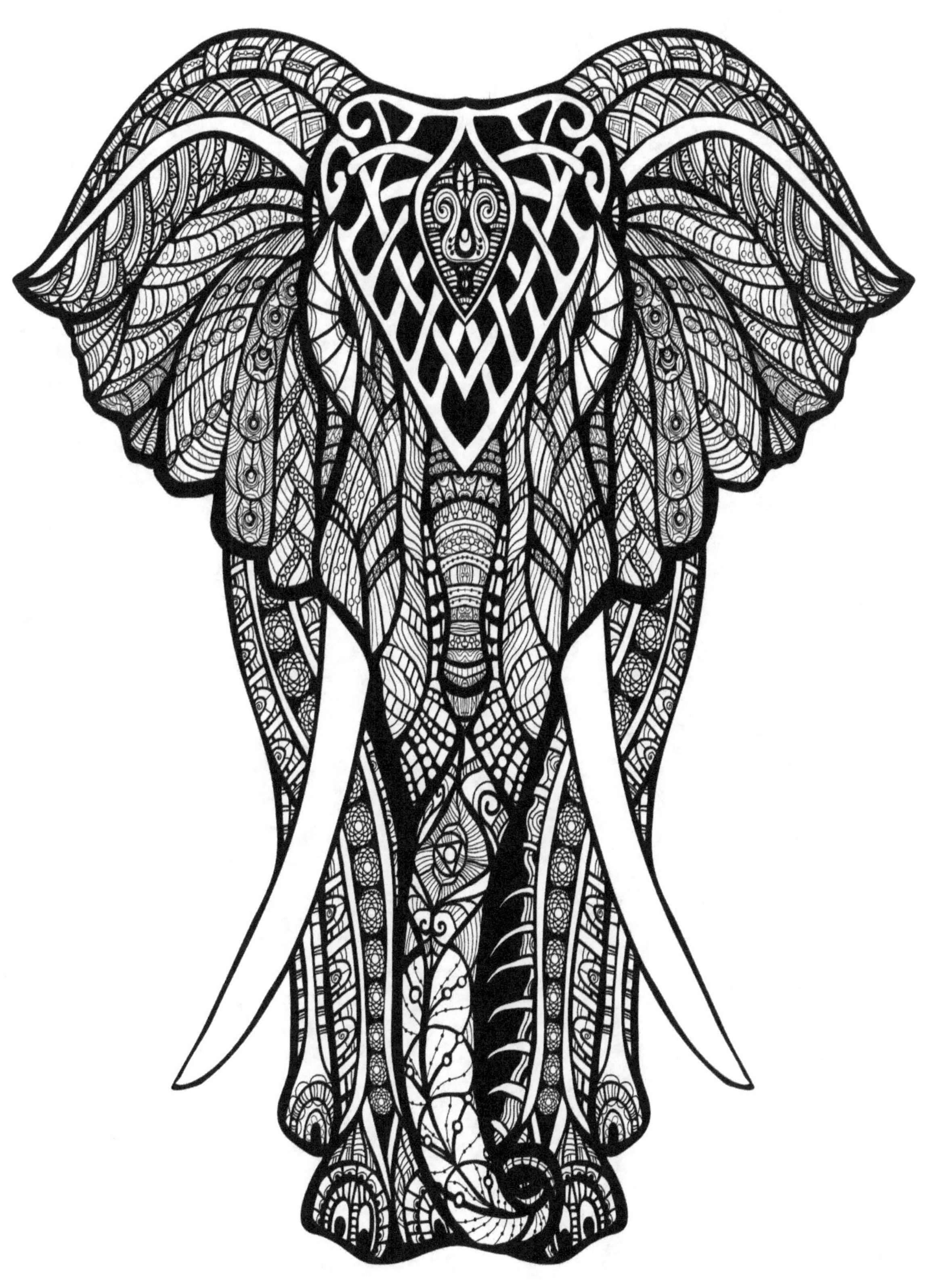

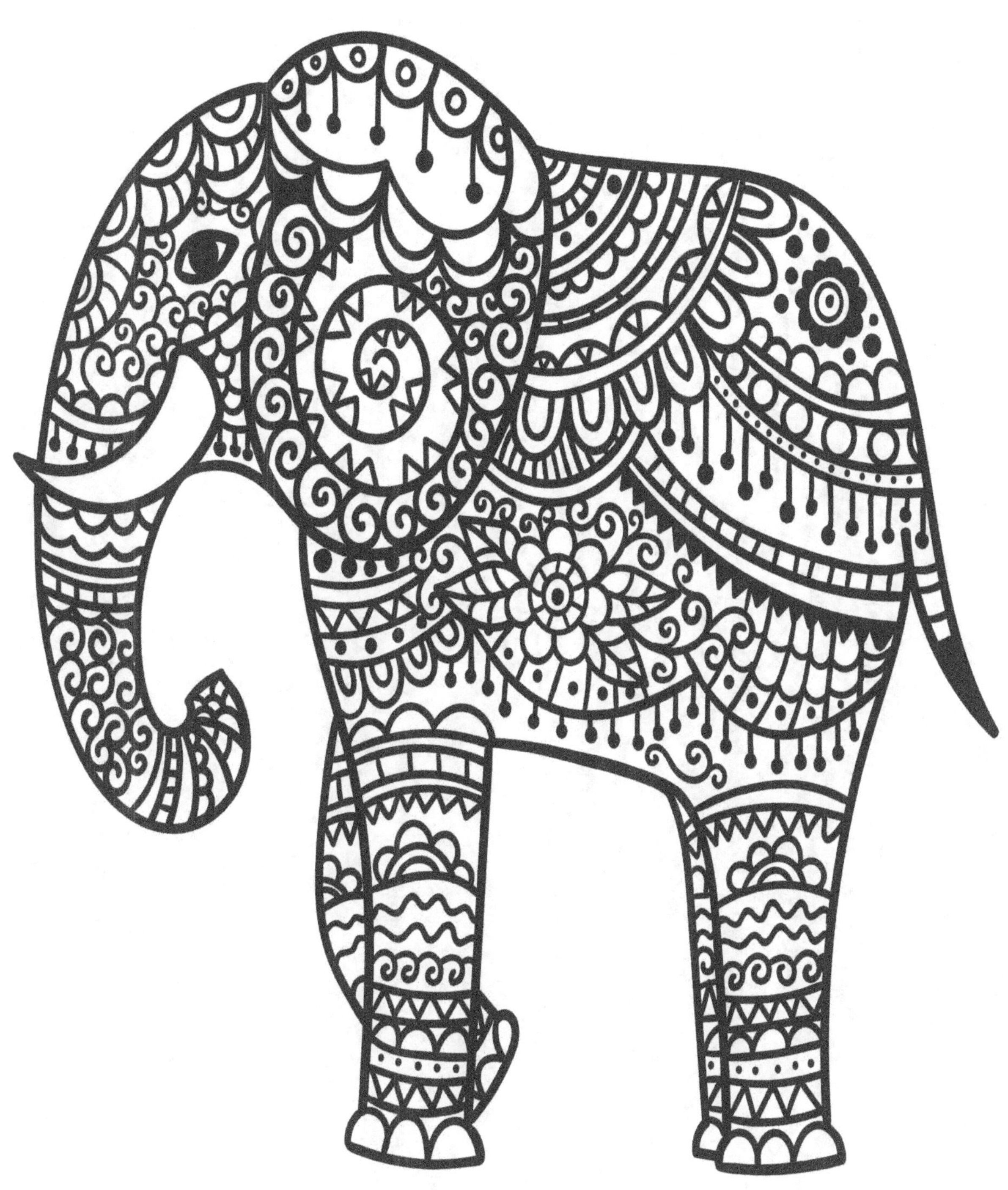

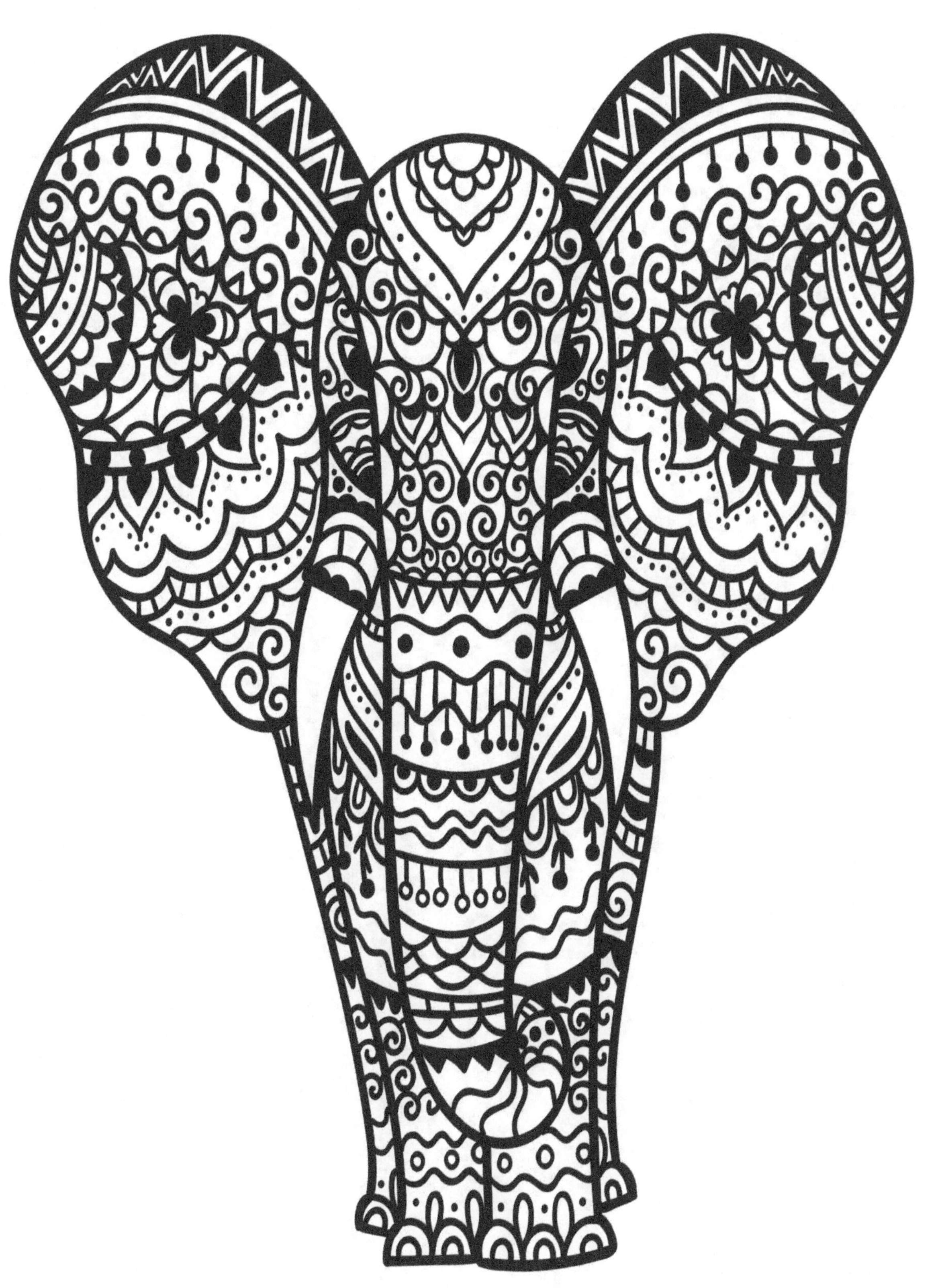

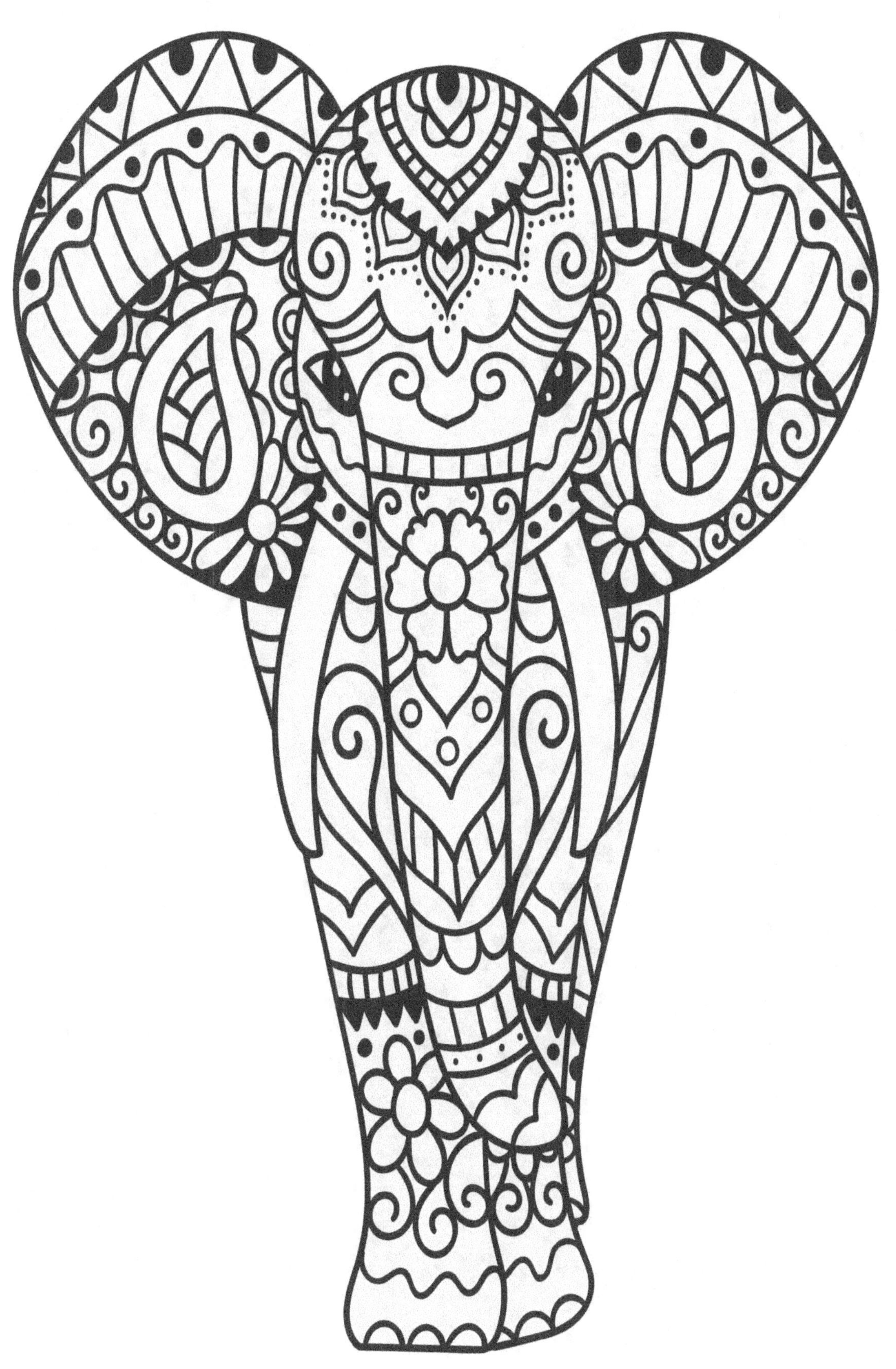

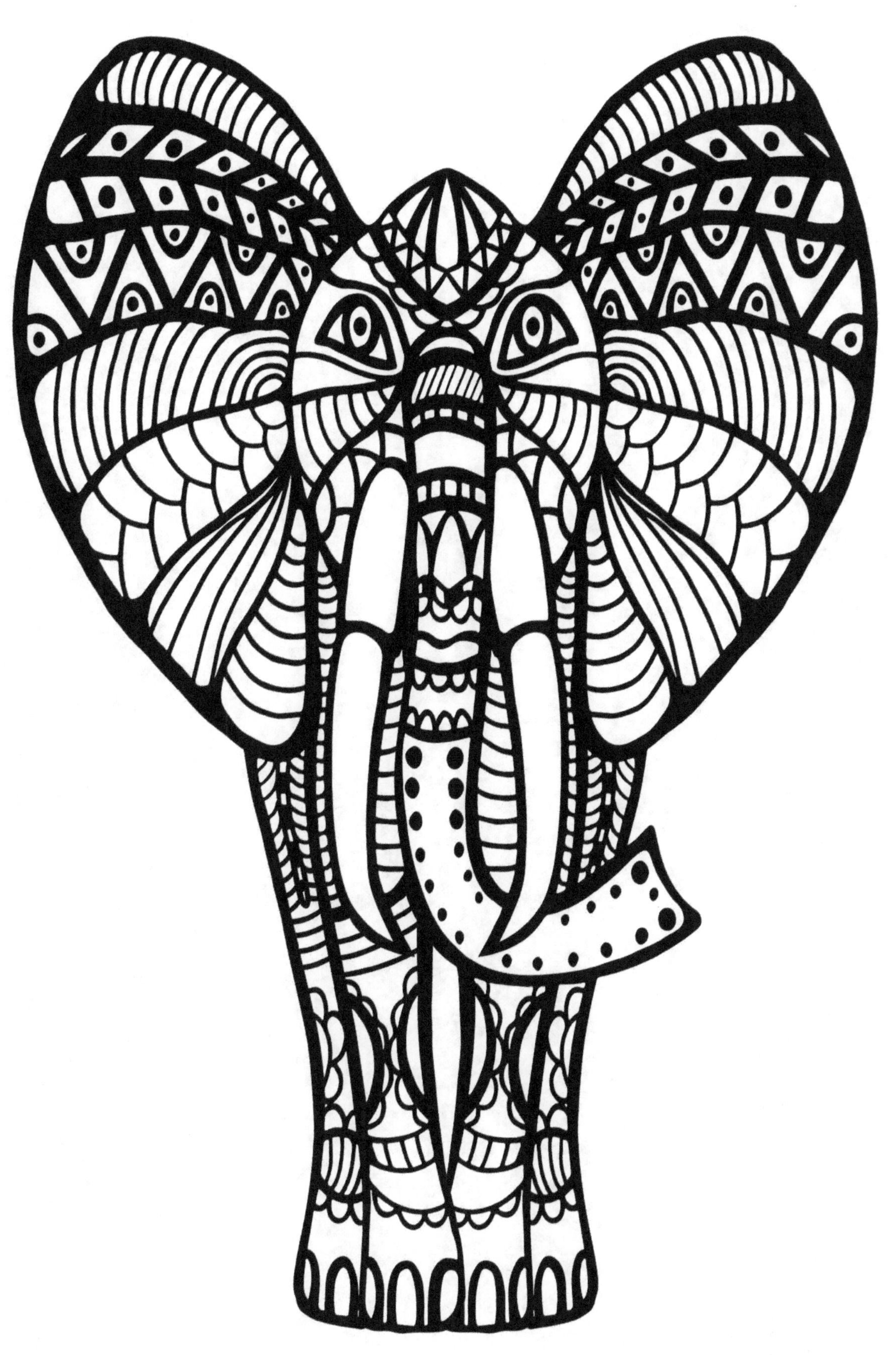

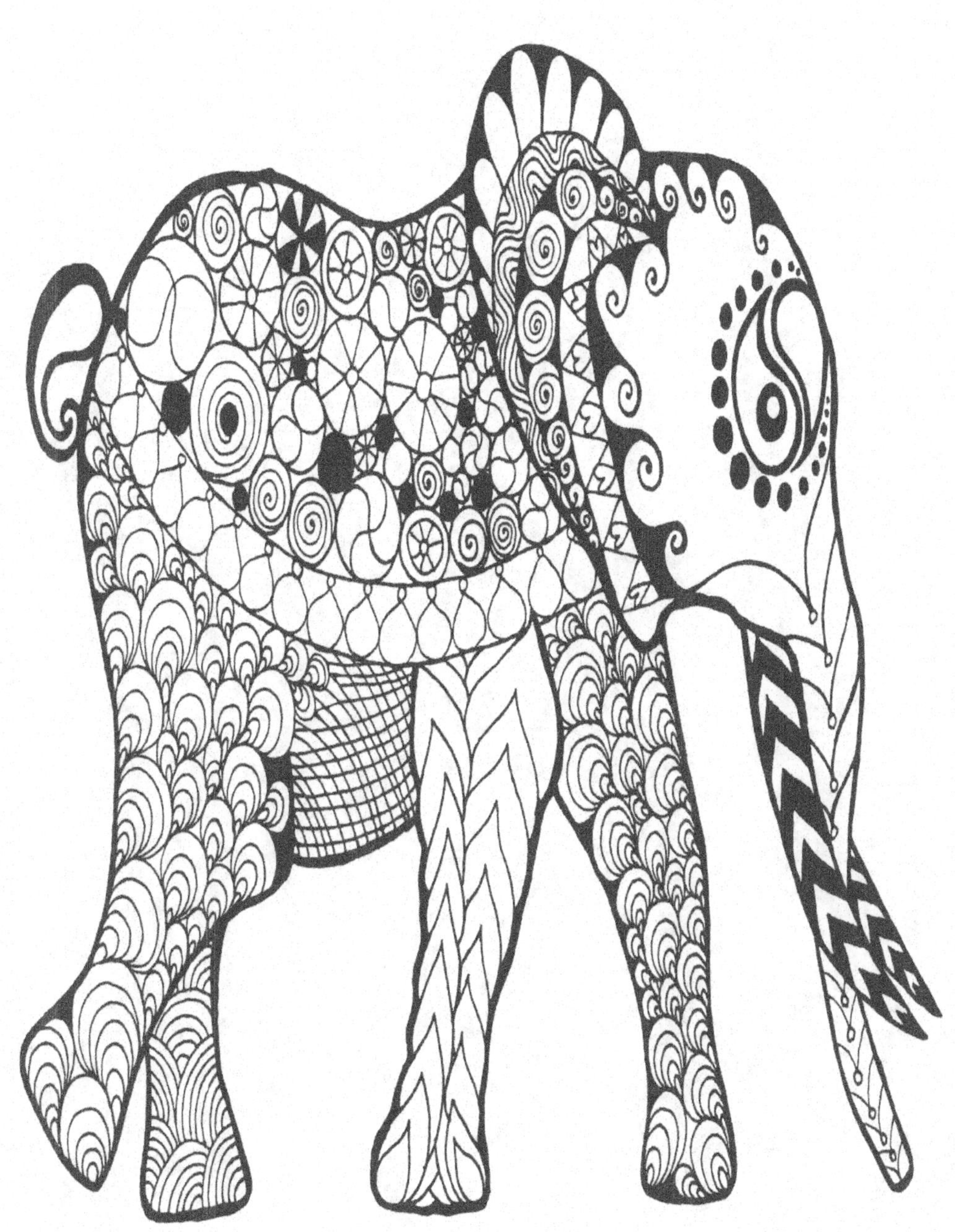

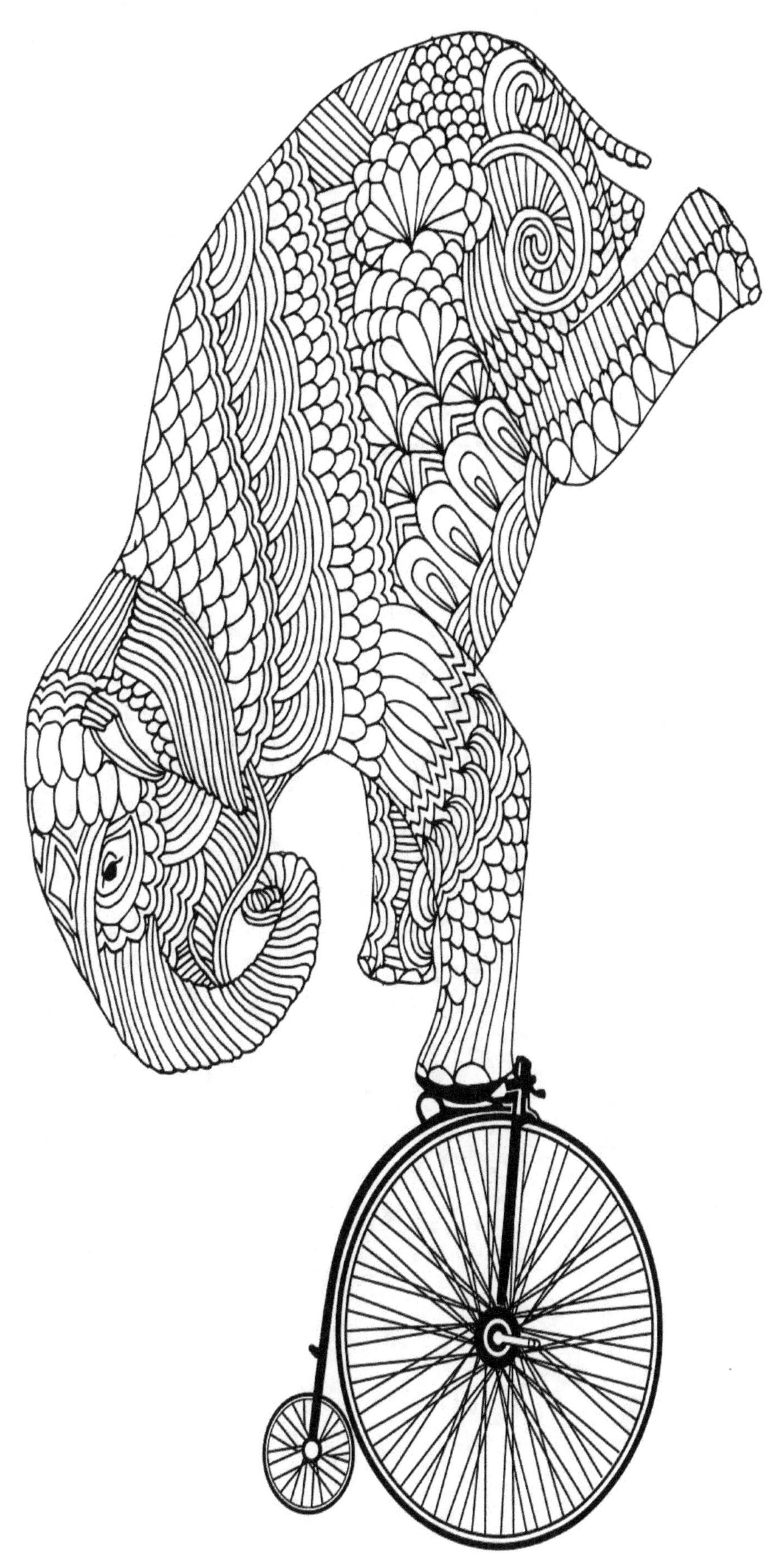

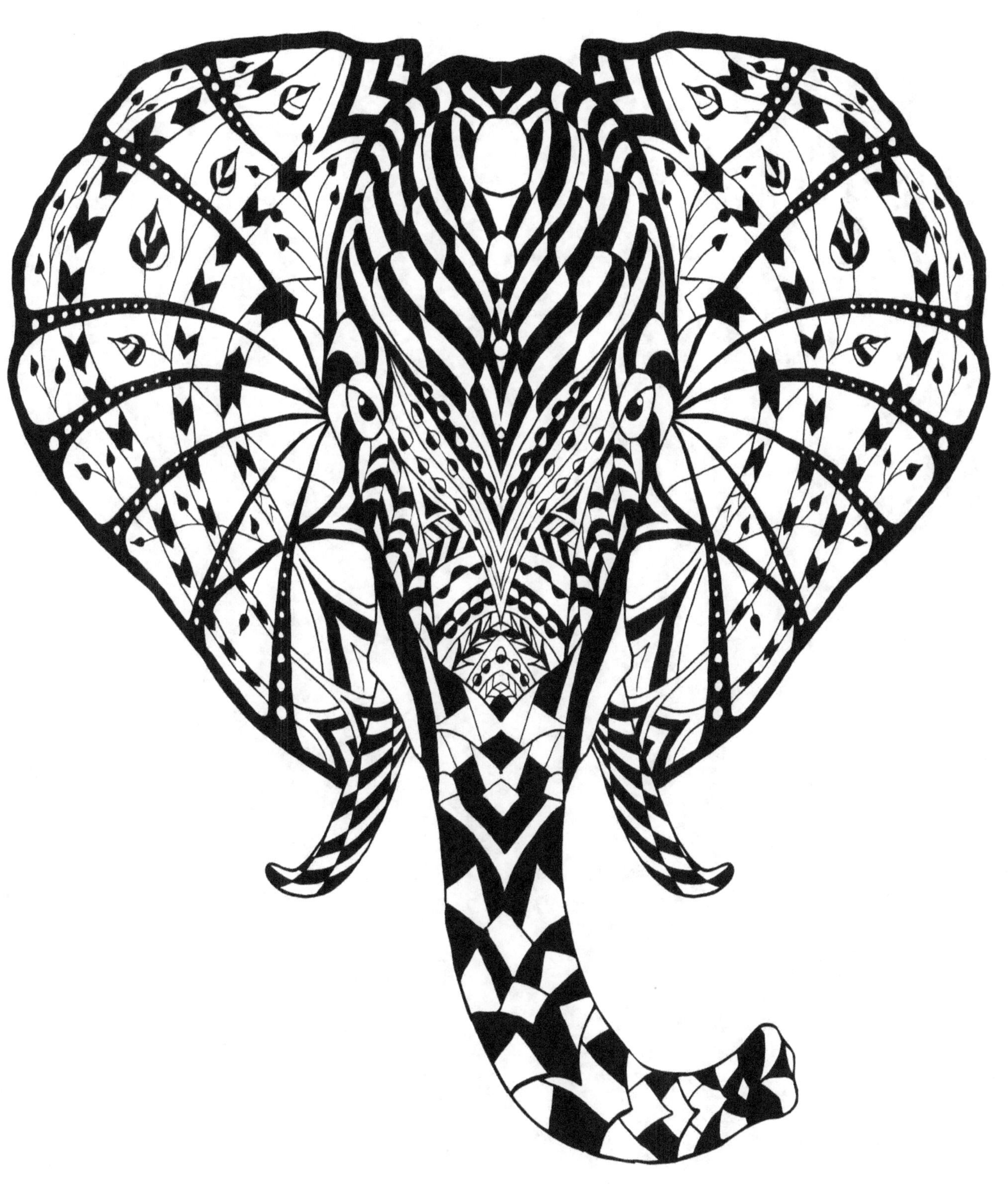

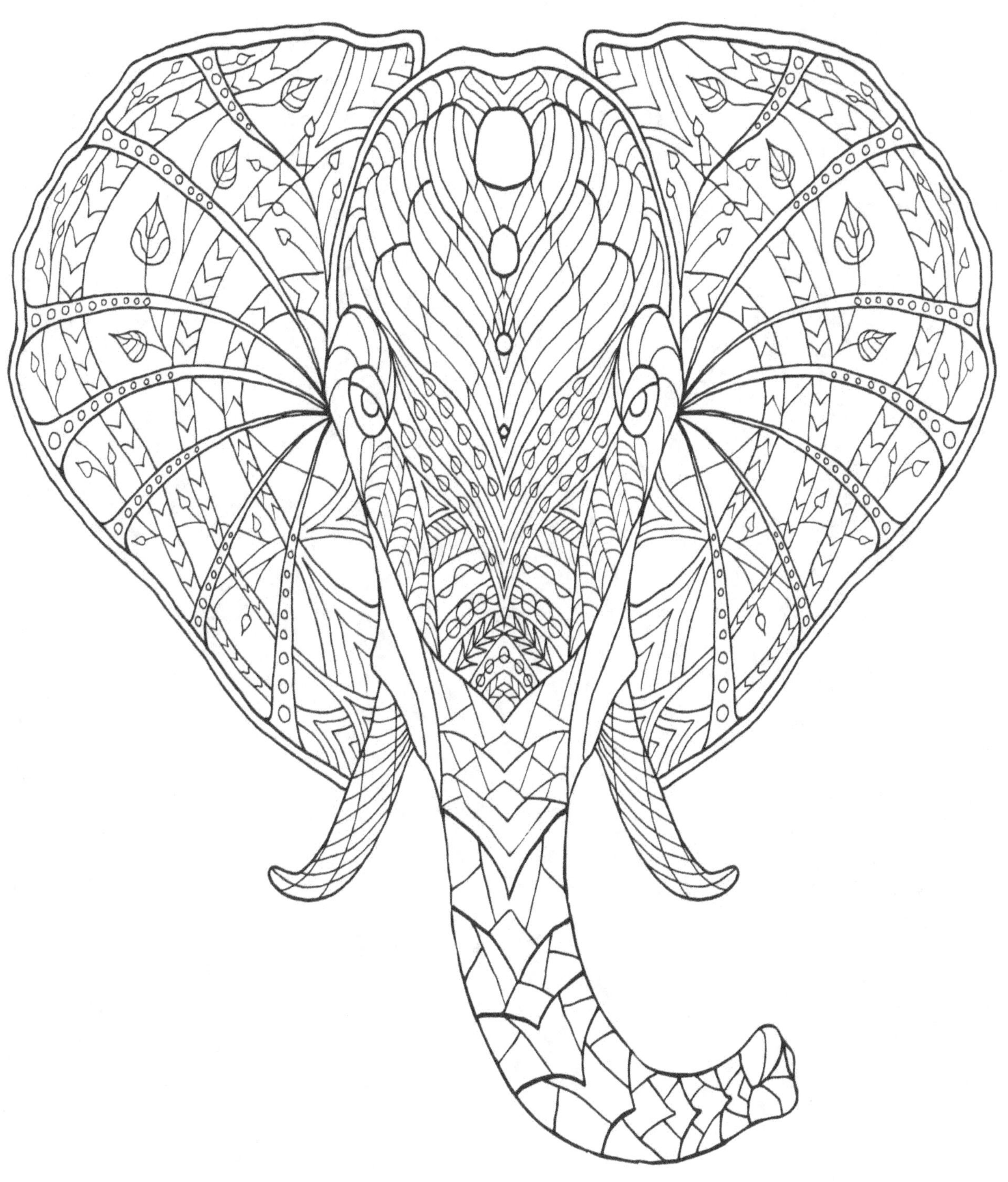

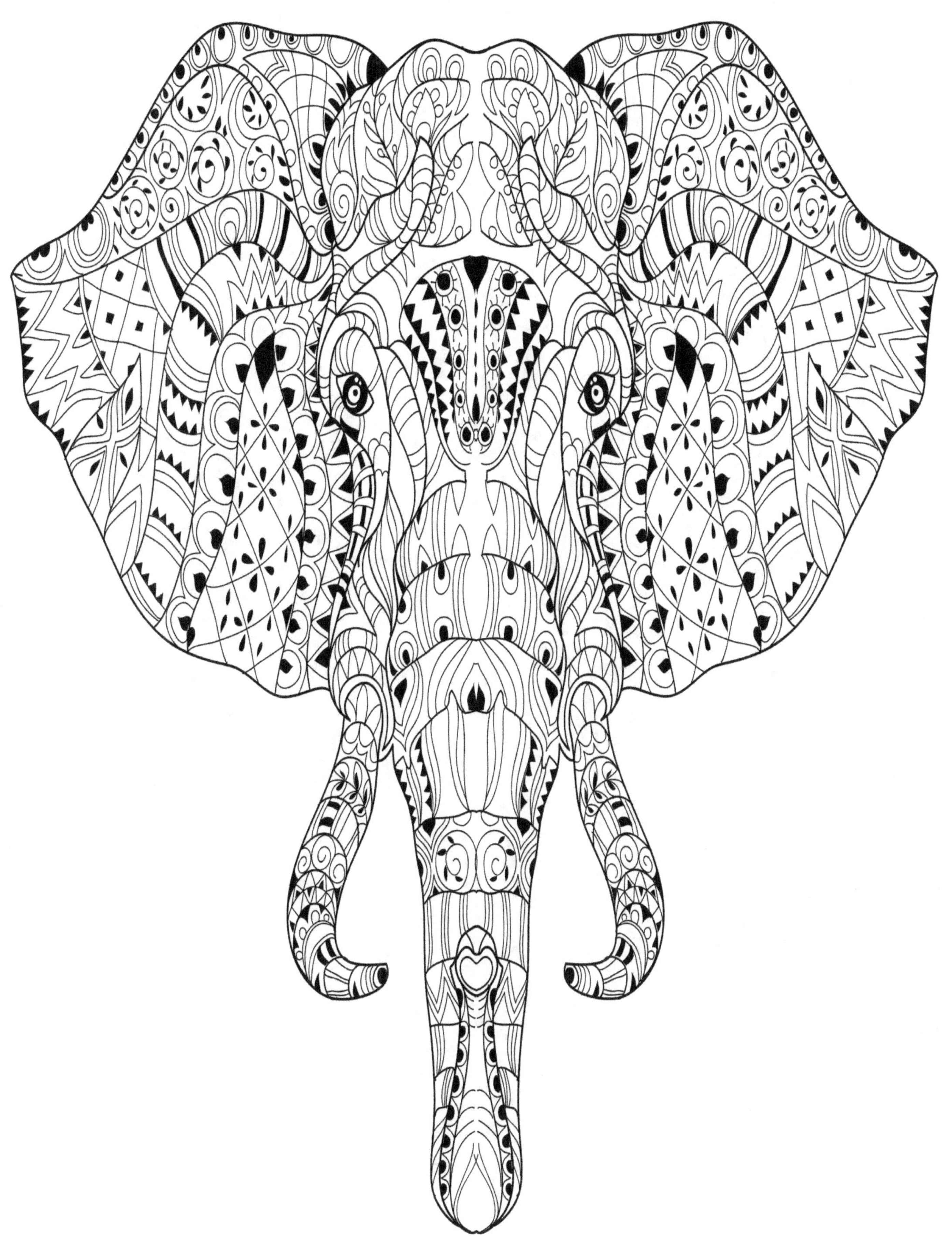

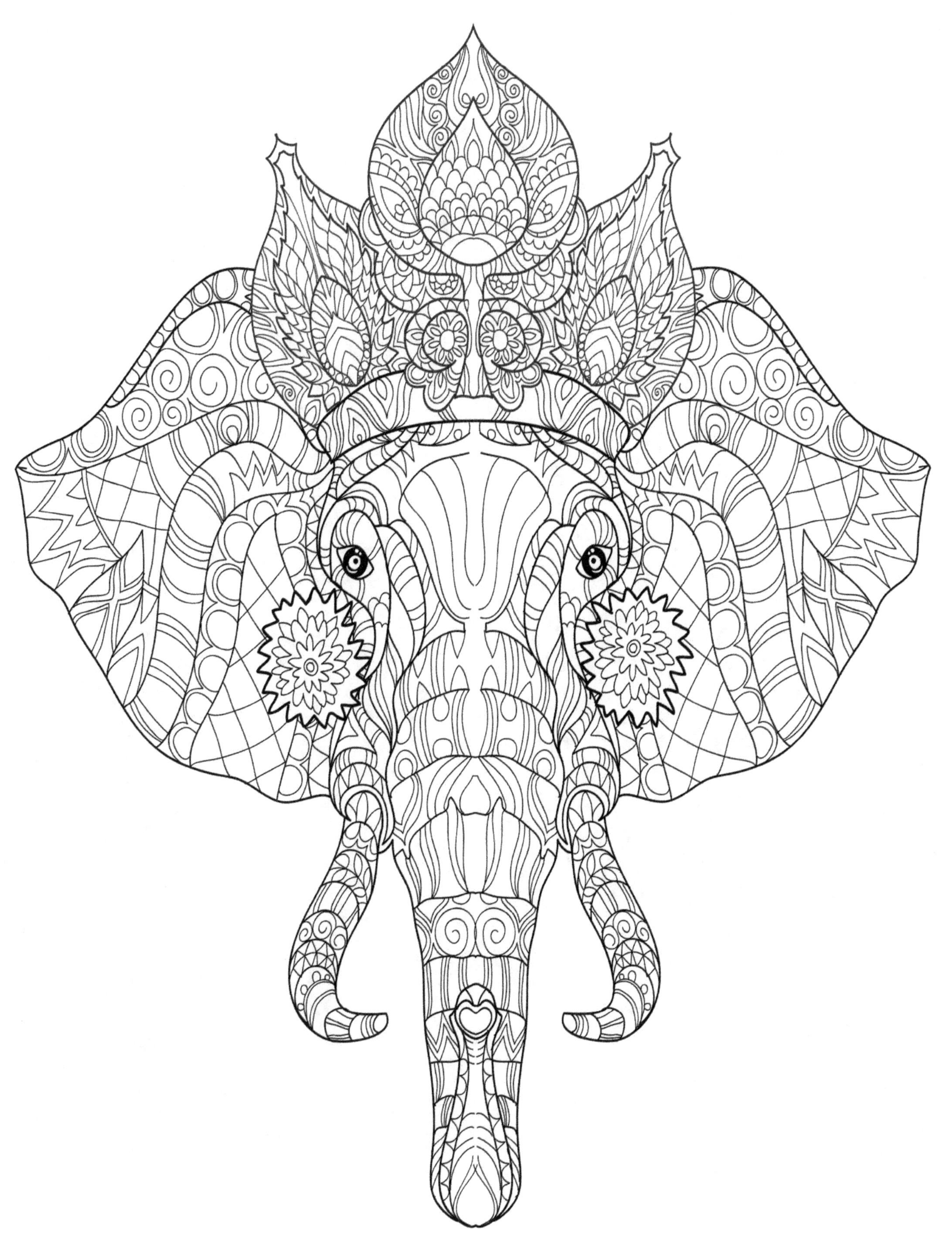

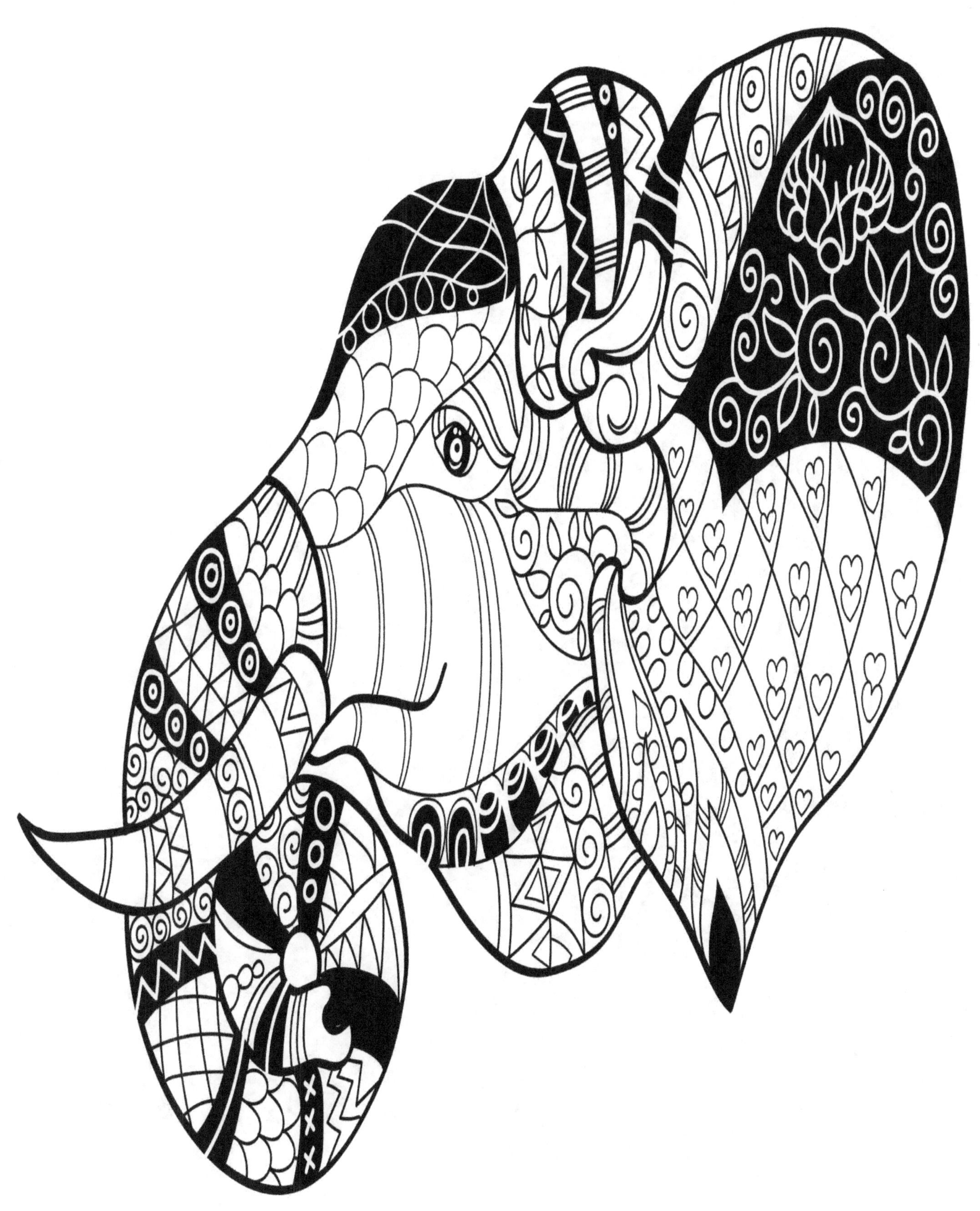

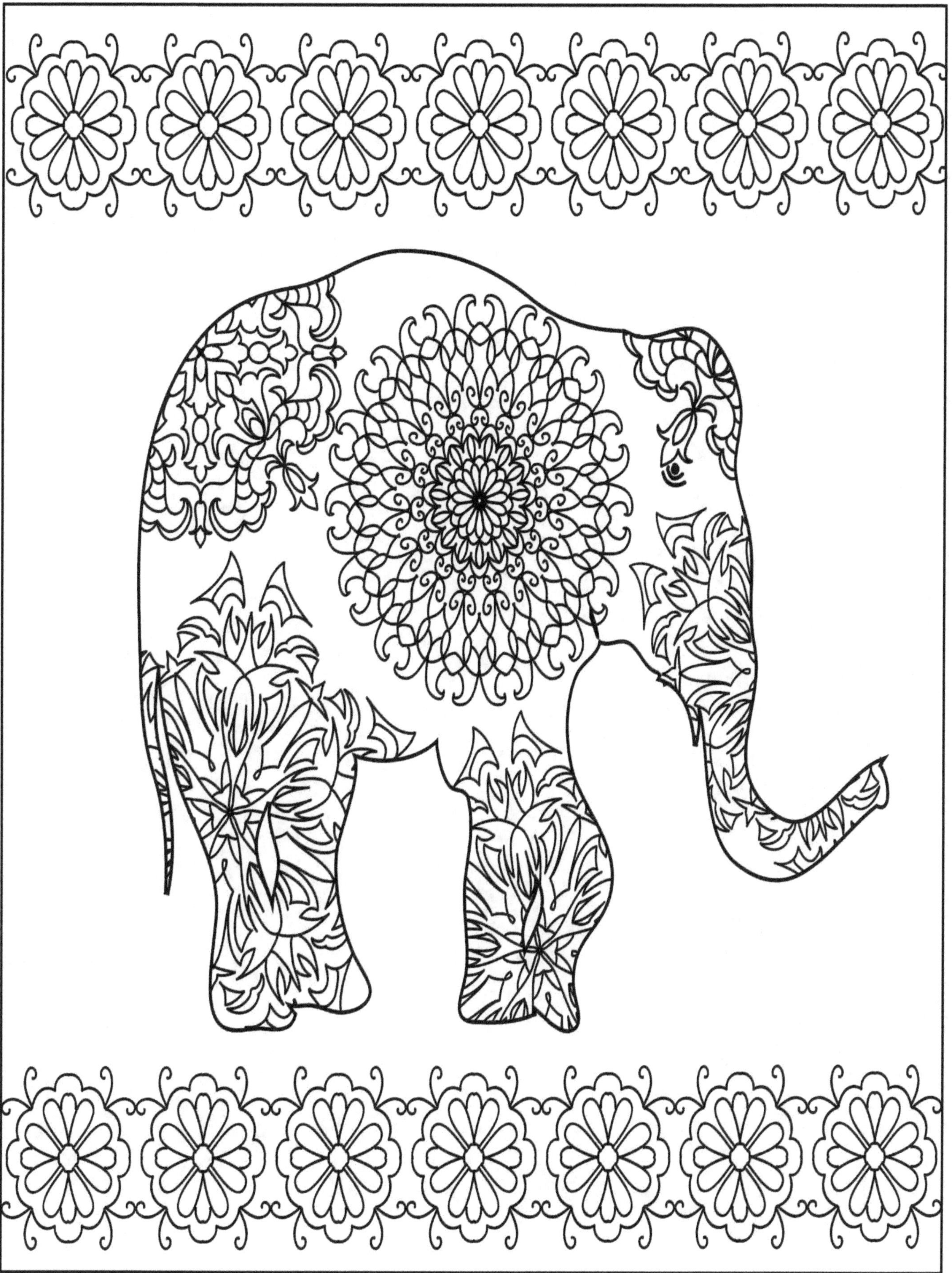

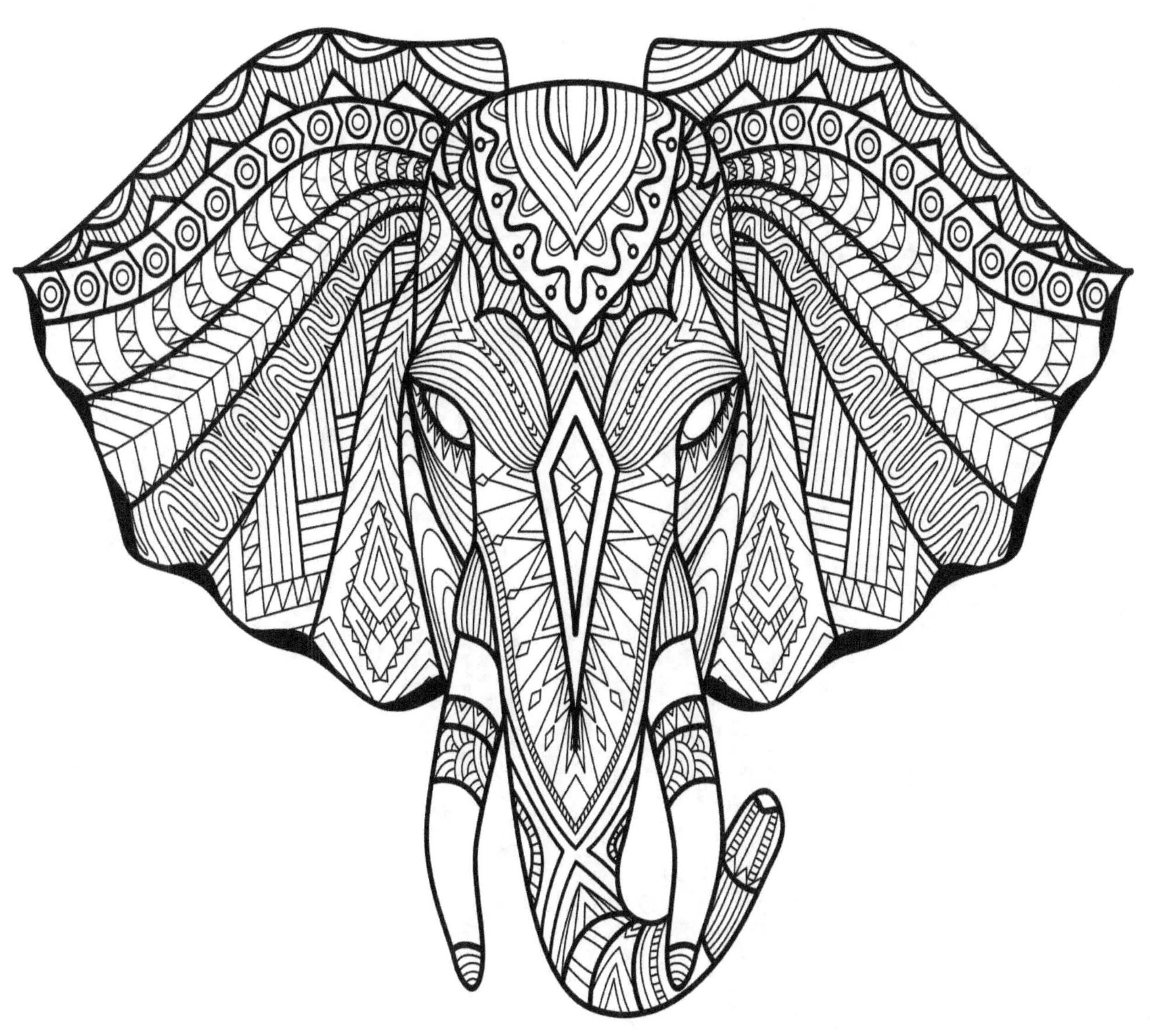

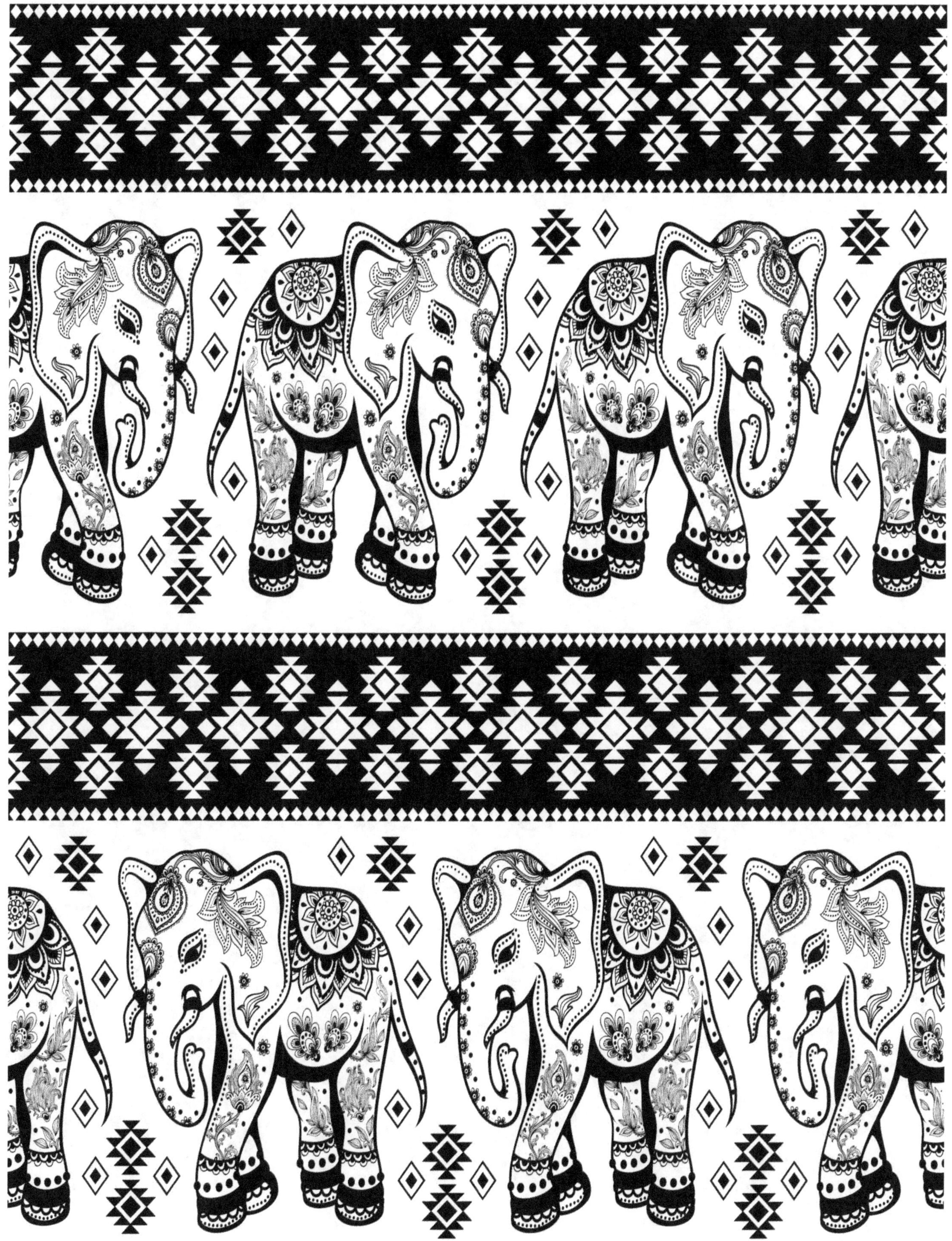

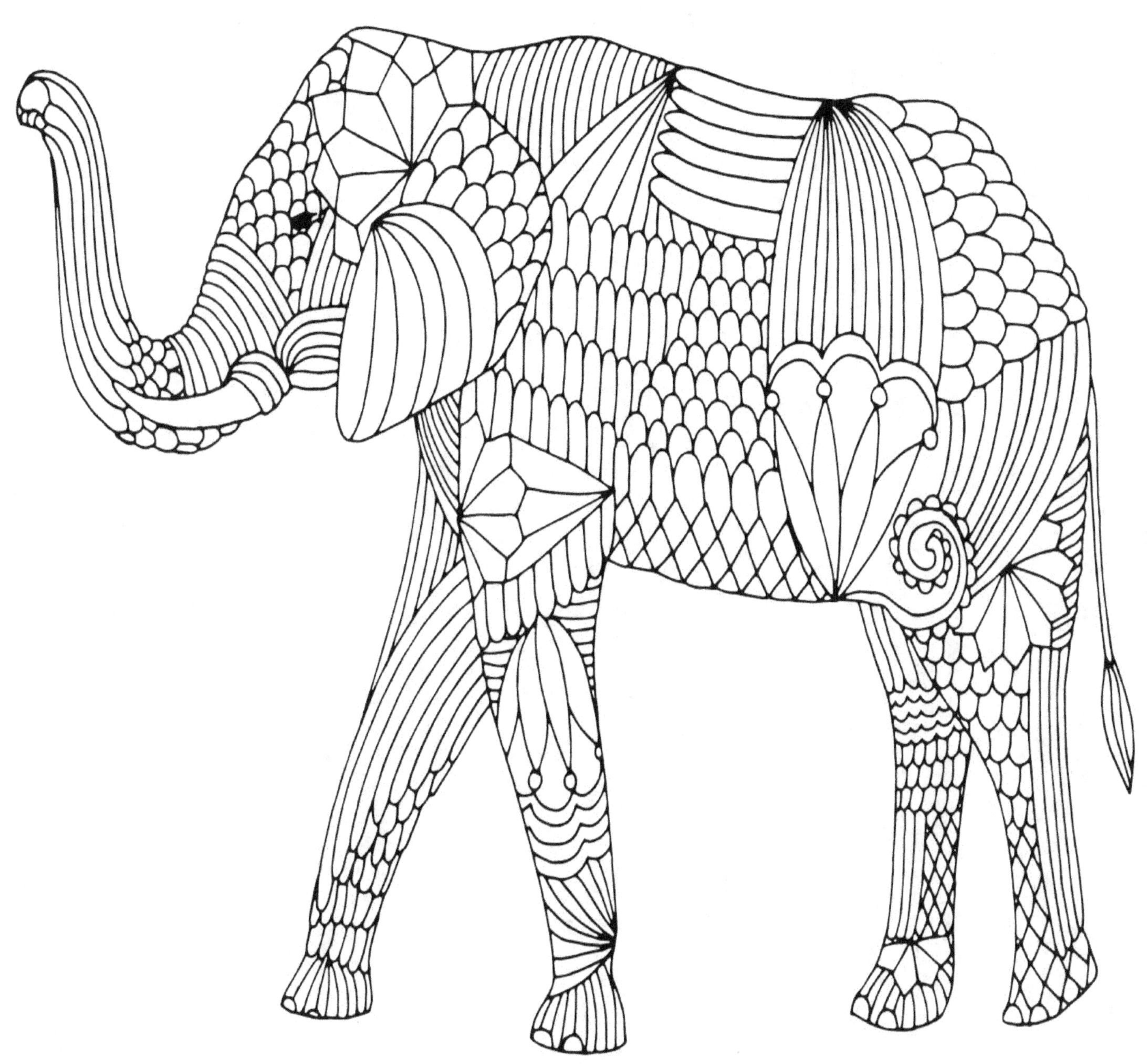

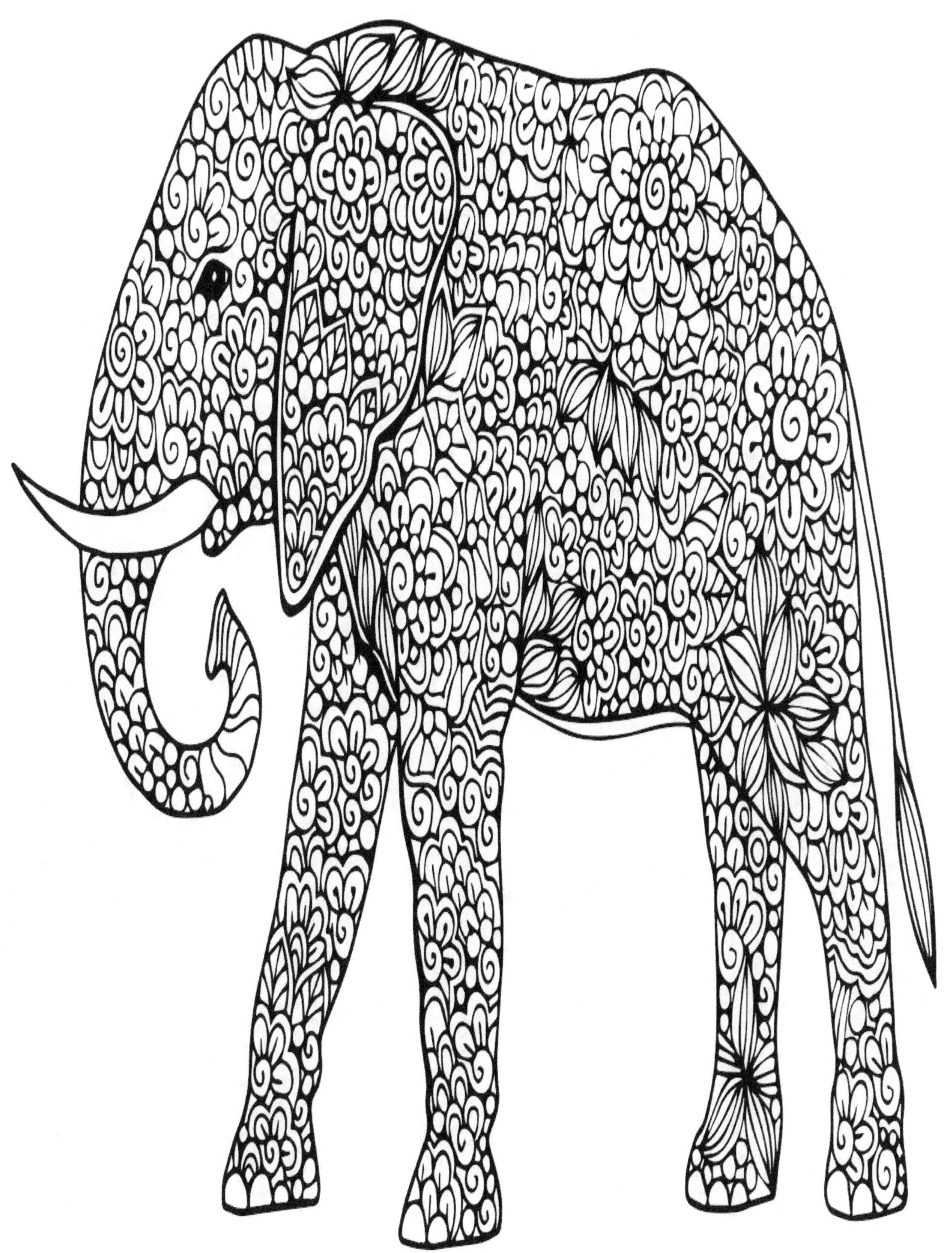

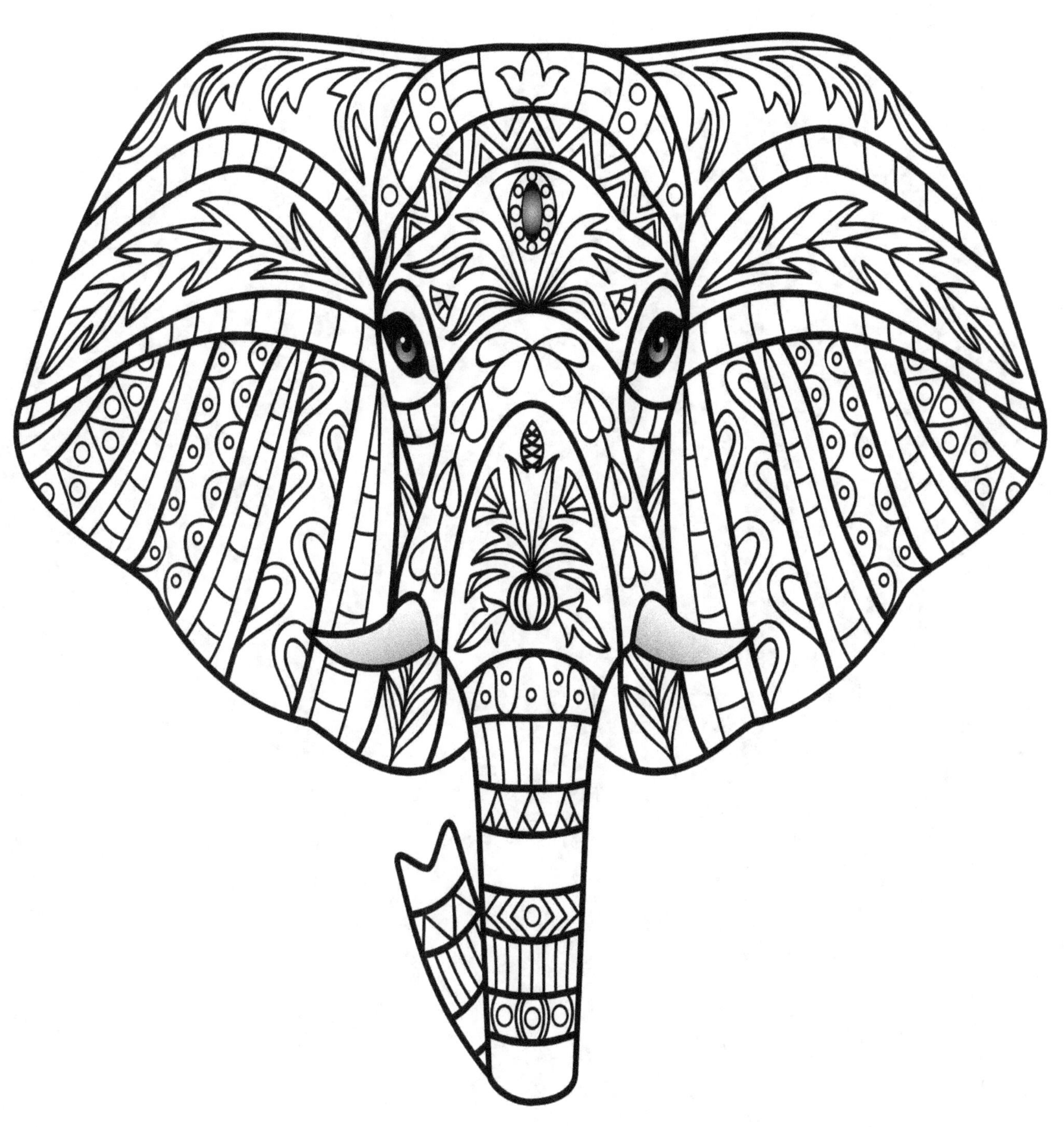

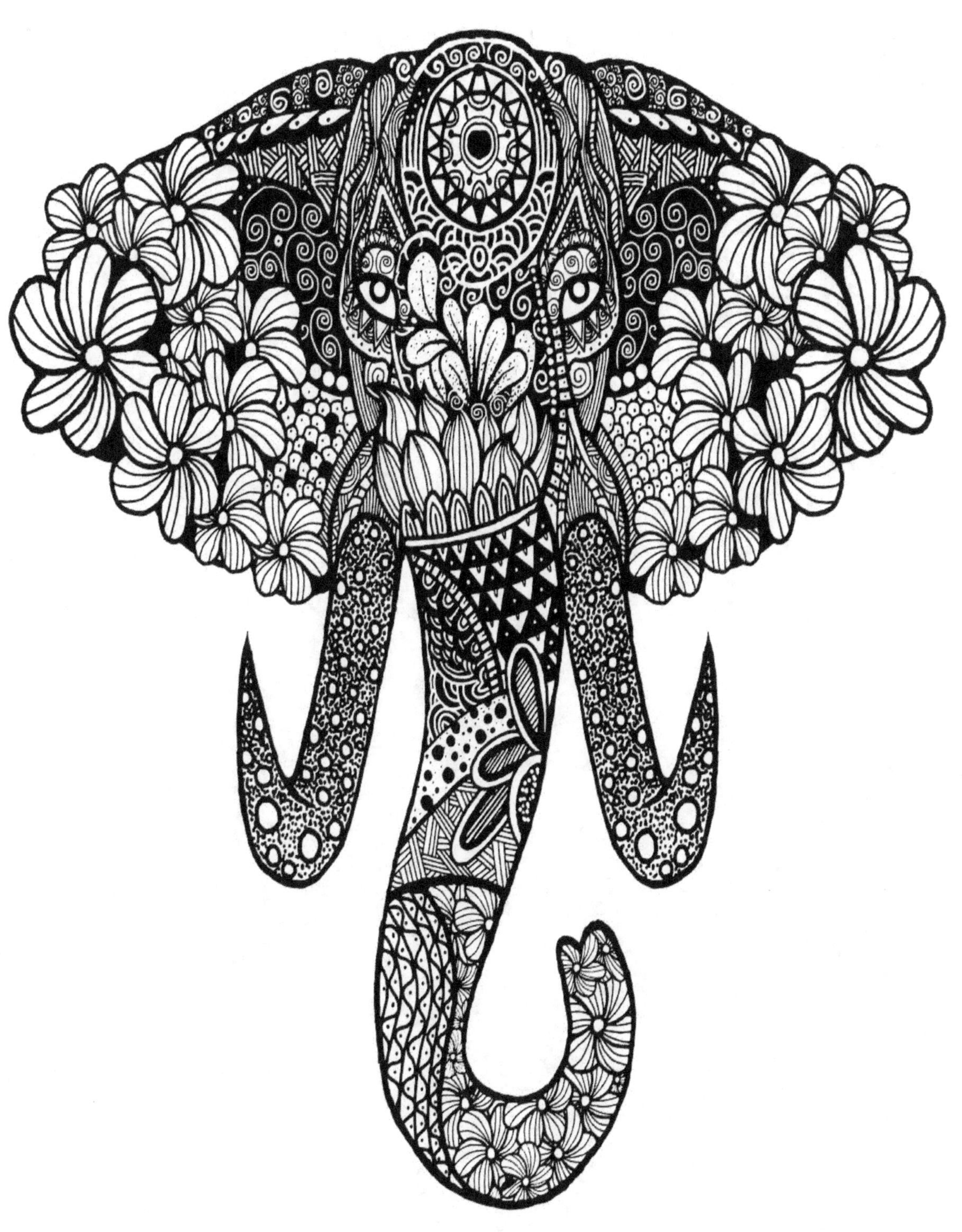

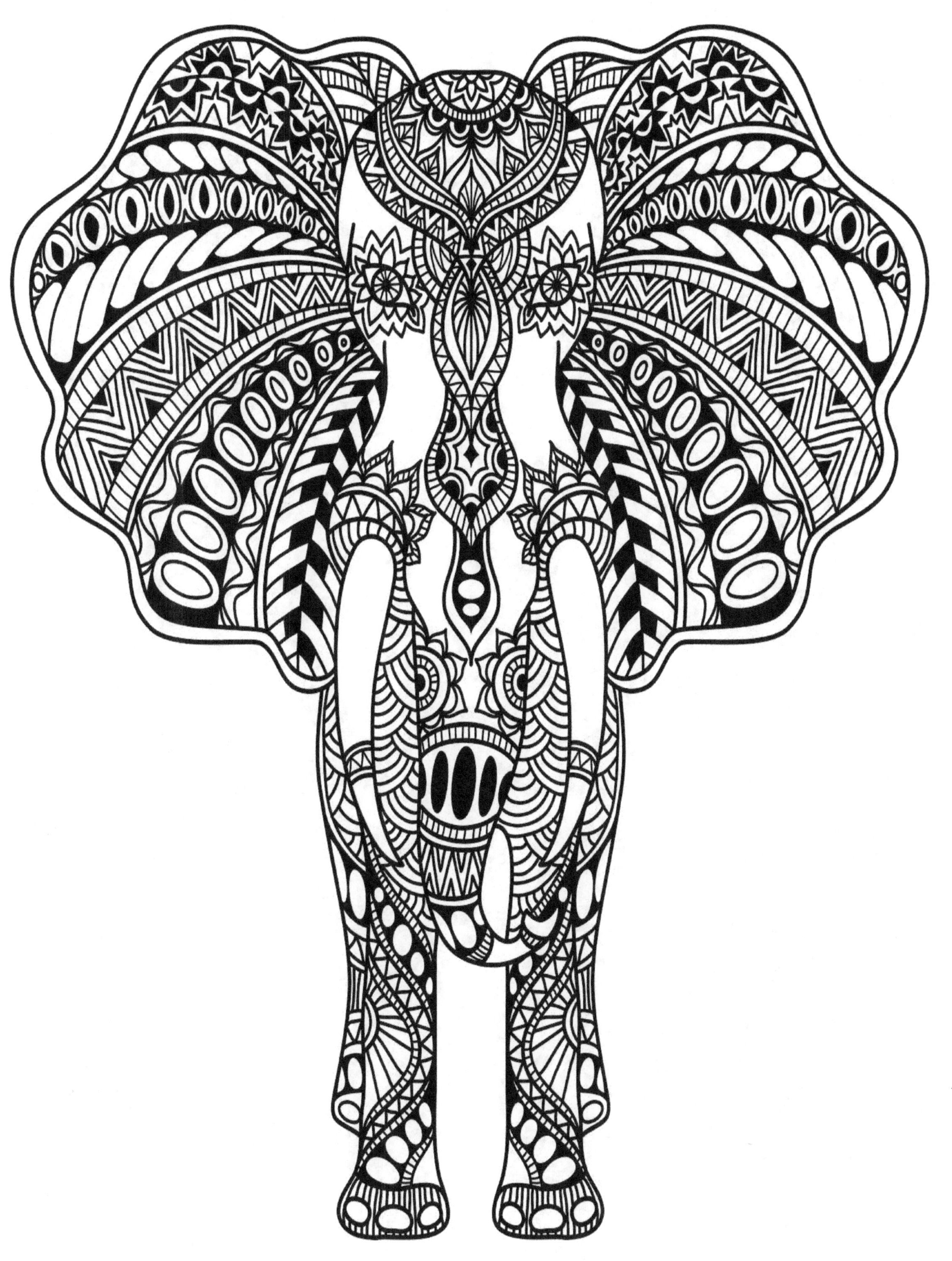

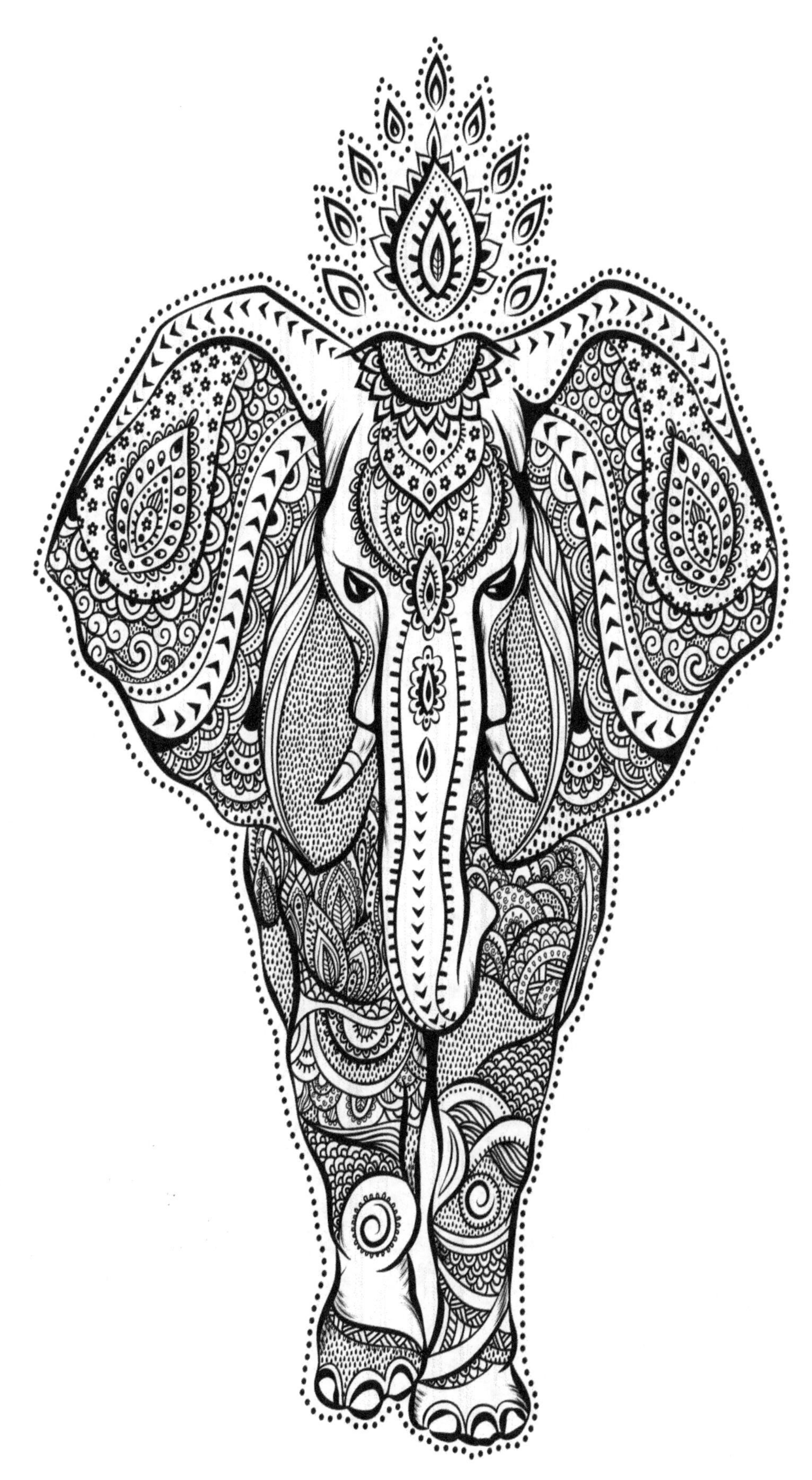

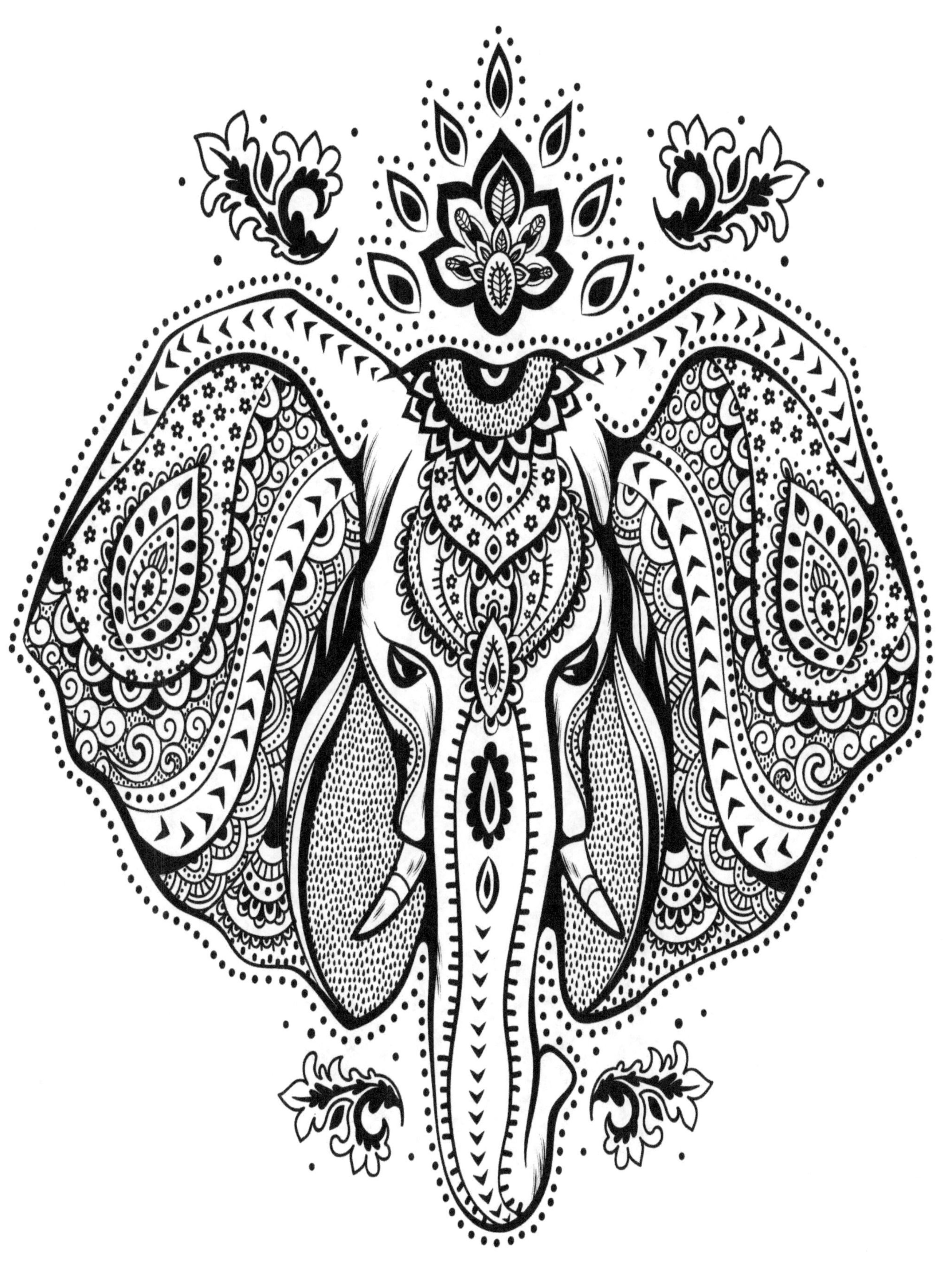

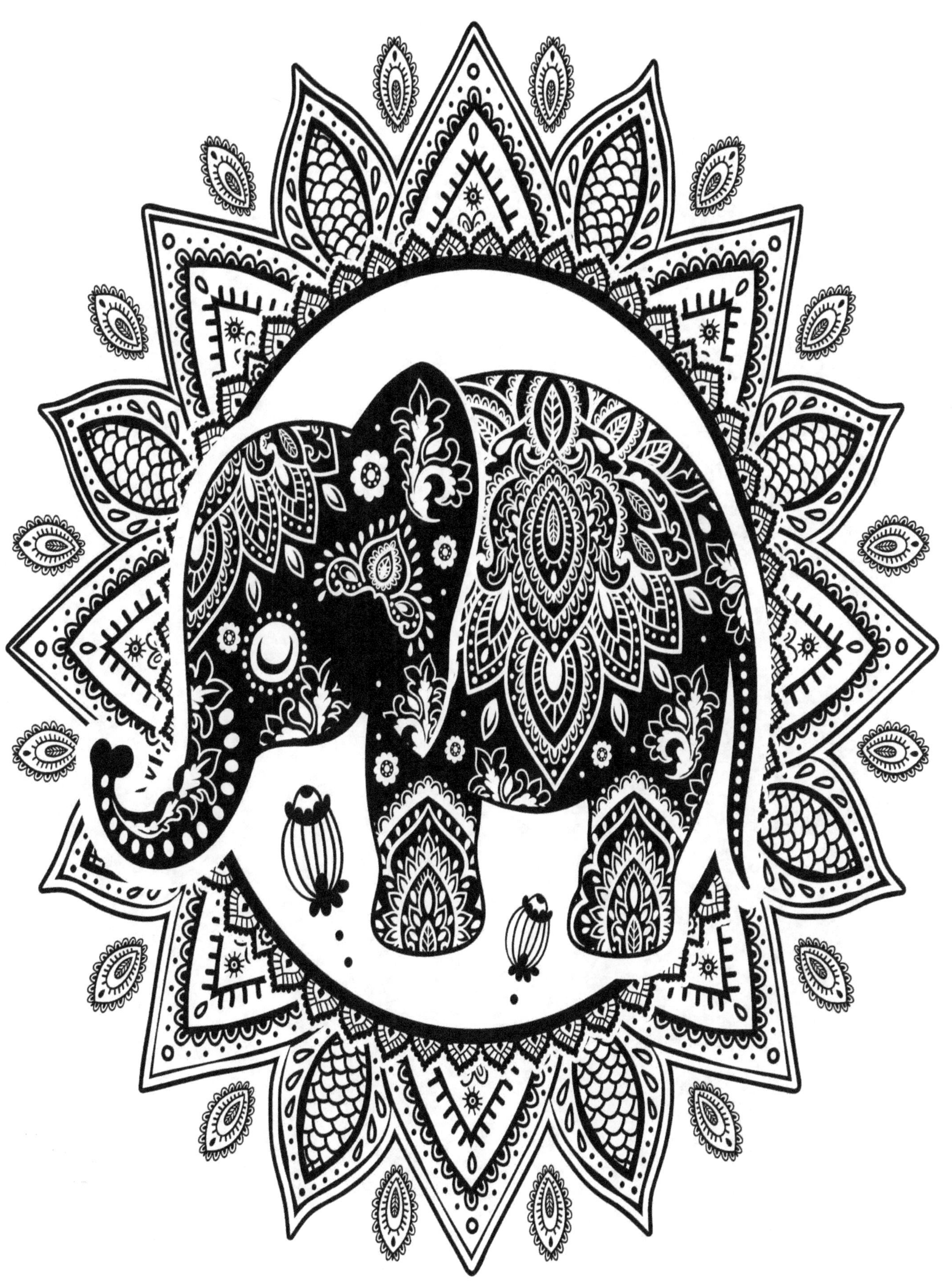

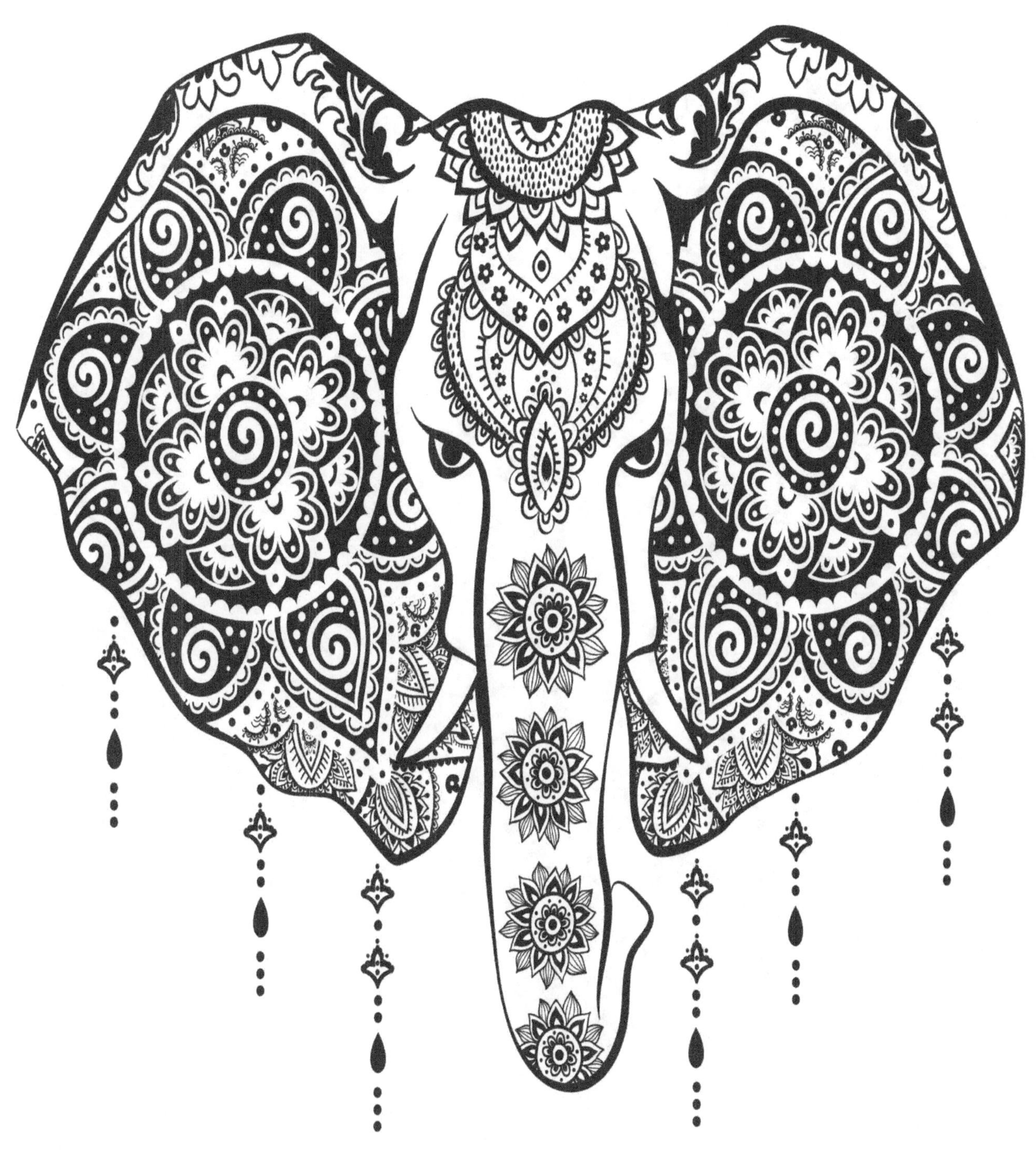

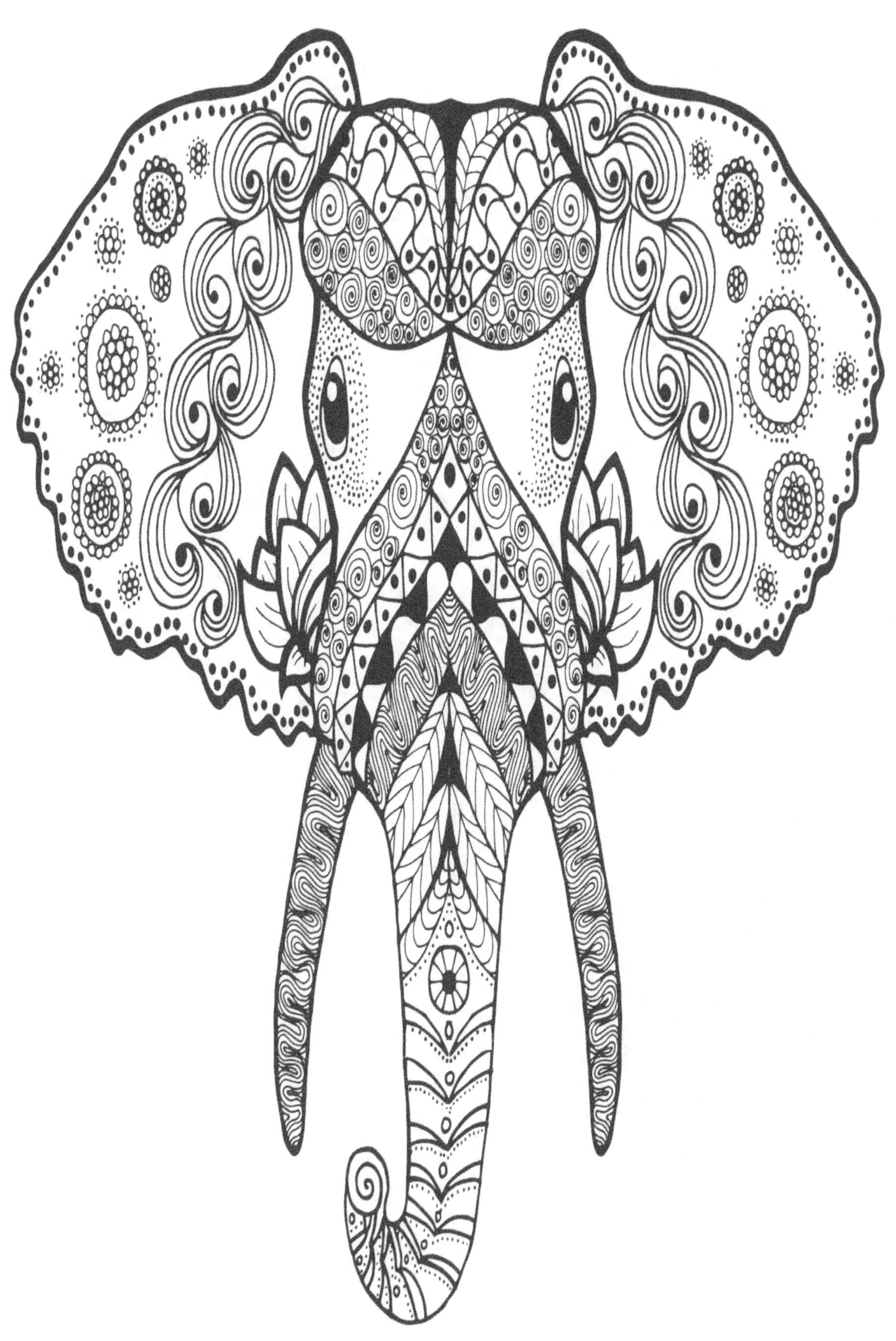

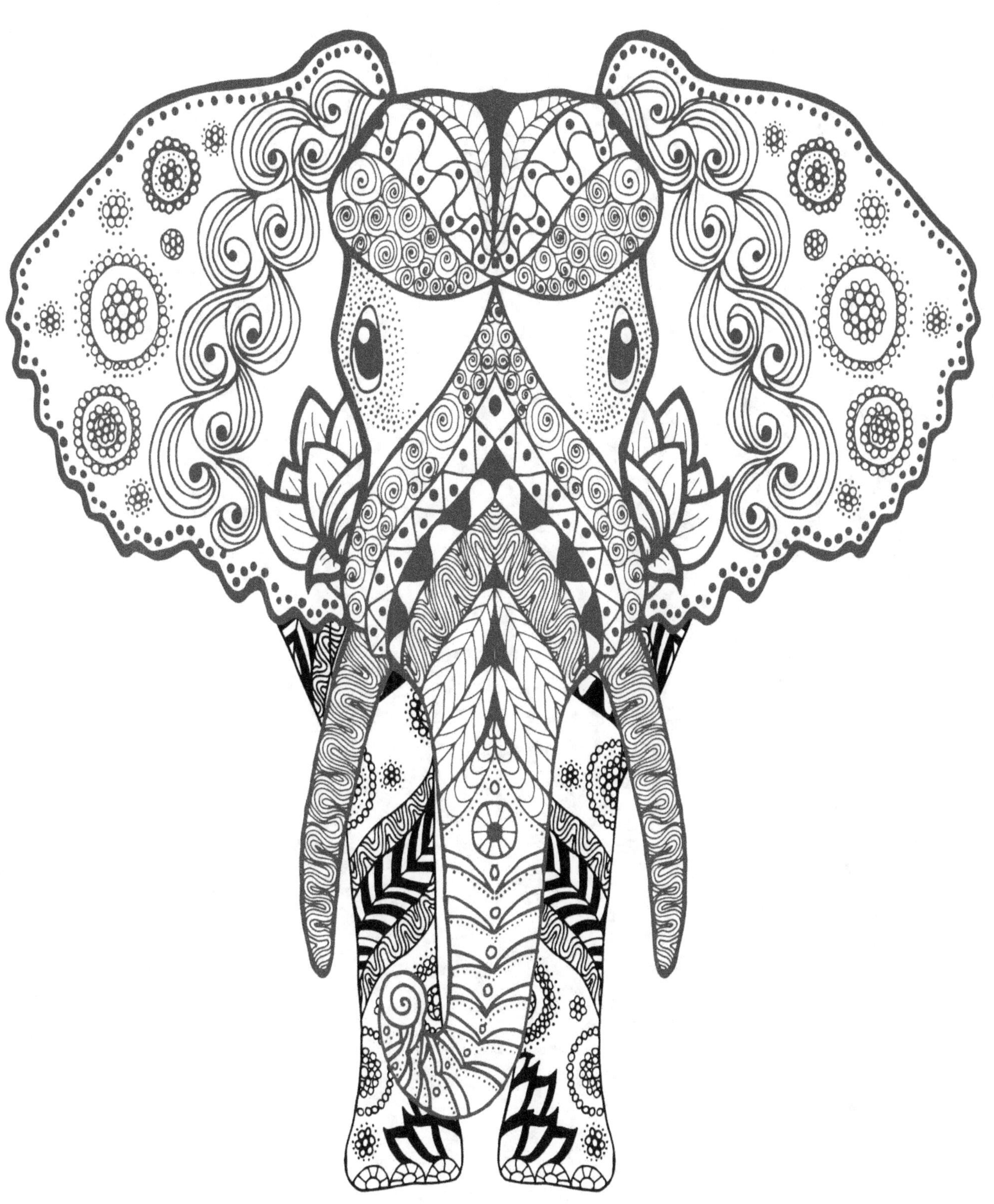

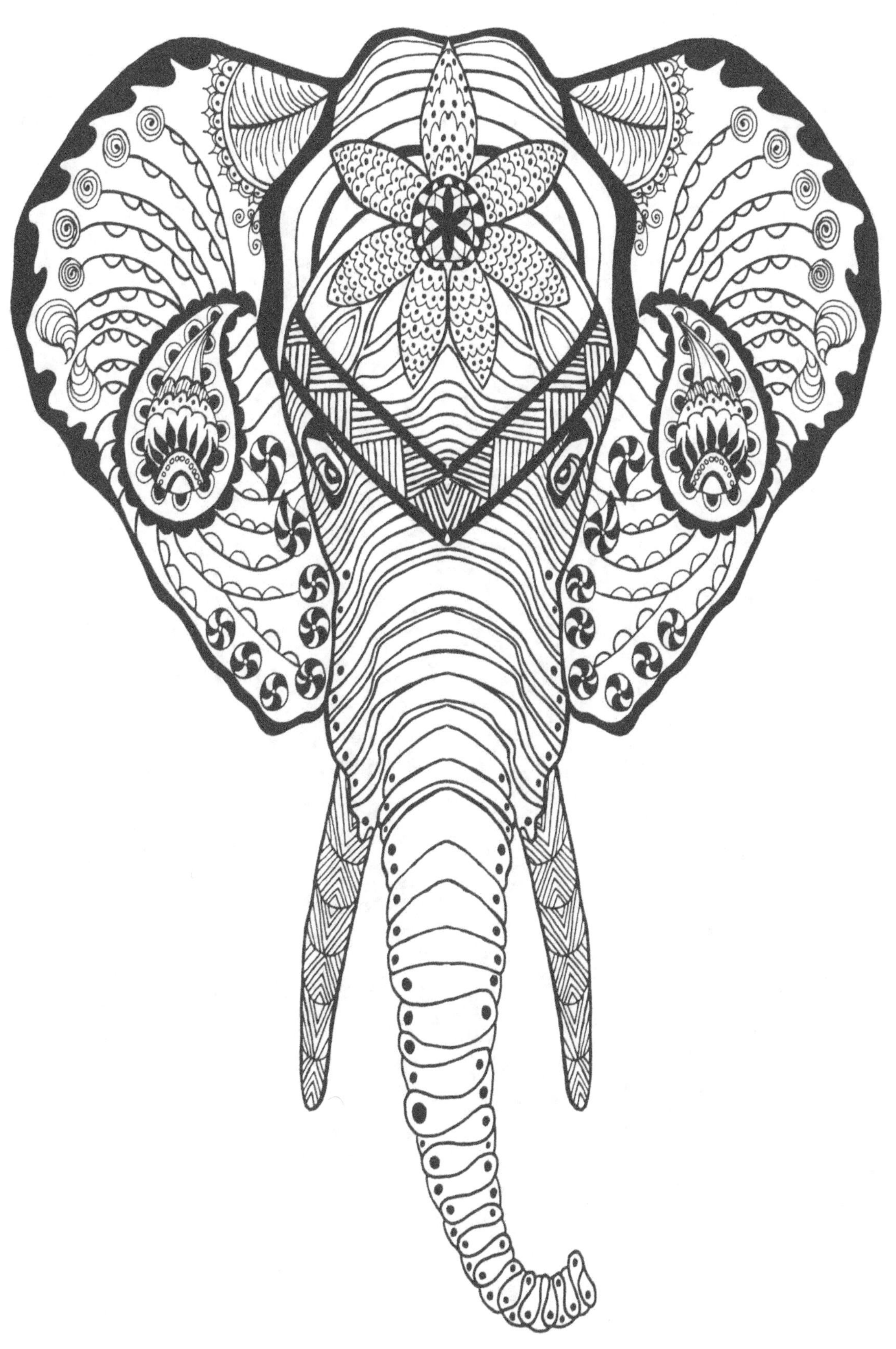